Read what others are s
Earth, the Forg

MW00833925

"Niki Collins-Queen's writing has a distinctively Hemingway-esque quality to it as she depends heavily on dialogue alternating with brief, vivid descriptions to propel her story forward. I feel deeply honored to have experienced her book."
—Pamela Stanescu, Editor & Educator

"Niki Collins-Queen really knows how to tell a story. One's interest does not flag. One has the feeling of an author holding nothing back.
—Forrest Altman, Editor and Author

"*Earth, the Forgotten Temple* put into words what I feel and believe, but never tried to explain because many would not understand why I don't go to church on Sunday. They think I don't worship --- !"
—Pat Blanks, Librarian

"*Earth, the Forgotten Temple* was a joy to read, yet it will make the average person ask: Why haven't I done more? Her book would be of major interest to one who is seeking a spiritual connection outside the conventional church, but did not know where to look. Niki Collins-Queen's powers of description are excellent, and the conclusion of the book is perfect."
—Linda Mizelle, Educator

"I could not put *Earth, the Forgotten Temple* down, even when I had things to do. I wanted to keep reading."
—Kaye Wansley, Librarian

"I admire Niki Collins-Queen's courage in writing this book and sharing her personal struggles, challenges, fears and accomplishments. There are too few books about women in the wilderness."

—Dorothy Krakow, Therapist

"*Earth, the Forgotten Temple* is wonderfully delightful! I feel privileged and honored to have read Niki Collins-Queen's life story and adventures."

—Denise Lester, Educator

"*Earth, the Forgotten Temple* made me feel as though I had taken the trips myself. I really enjoyed the descriptions of the wilderness and the animals—they became very visual to me. It was good to be able to experience nature without actually being there."

—Yvonne Elkins, Social Worker

"It is a privilege to read a true story about exploring nature. *Earth, the Forgotten Temple* is a true to life adventure story for nature lovers."

—Louis Lowery, Master Gardener

"Niki Collins-Queen was able to nurture others from learning how to self-mother by receiving nurture from nature."

—Ann Hibbard, Massage Therapist

EARTH,
THE FORGOTTEN TEMPLE

A Spirit Quest in the Wilderness

Niki Collins-Queen

Foreword by James Palmer

Impala Press
Forsyth, Georgia

Author's Note

Some names and identifying details of individuals mentioned in the book have been changed to protect their privacy.

Earth, the Forgotten Temple: Copyright © 2000 by Niki Collins-Queen. All rights reserved. Printed in the United States of America. No part of this book may be used or reproduced without written permission except in the case of brief quotations embodied in critical articles and reviews.

IMPALA PRESS
1387 Boxankle Road
Forsyth, Ga 31029
Phone and Fax (912) 992-9063

FIRST EDITION
First Printing, 2000

Publisher's Cataloging-in-Publication
(*Privid by Quality Books, Inc.*)

Collins-Queen, Niki.
  Earth, the forgotten temple: a spirit quest in the wilderness / Niki Collins-Queen ; foreword by James Palmer. -- 1st ed.
  p. cm.
  LCCN: 99-94538
  ISBN: 0-9672112-0-4

  1. Collins-Queen, Niki--Journeys. 2. Spiritual Biography 3. Earth--Religious aspects. 4. Vision quests. 5. Cohutta Wilderness (Ga. and Tenn.)--Description and travel. 6. Florida--Description and travel. 7. Bahamas--Description and travel. I. Title.
  BL73.C65A3 2000   291.4'092
                          QBI 99-1573

Foreword

Life is an adventure, if you only know how to live it. Niki Collins-Queen has discovered that secret. I first met her after she had completed a one-woman adventure in the Everglades. In writing a story about her, I referred to her beliefs of spirituality and their connection with nature as the Church of the Great Outdoors.

"It's very much like getting to know a loved one," she told me. "The more time you spend with them, the more your love deepens."

But her love of the outdoors is only one part of this unique person. Most of us find it very difficult to open up and reveal who we really are. Out secret selves, often full of fears and uncertainties, can become a burden. Collins-Queen is disarming in her ability to show you her true self. She's now combined that ability, her love for the outdoors and her adventurous spirit into a book.

Earth, the Forgotten Temple, recounts the life story of a woman in the wilderness. But the journey far surpasses the physical. It's also her quest for truth, for life's meaning and for the spirituality that should guide all of us in our day-to-day pursuits.

It's a brave book by a brave woman who has endured the dangers nature can offer as well as the joys it brings those who take the time to fully appreciate its wonder.

You can enjoy the book for the shared experience from someone bold enough to do what many of us probably dream about doing, striking out on an adventure. But its essence is that of a quest—one person seeking the true spirit of nature and God.

—James Palmer, Metro Editor, The Macon Telegraph

Acknowledgments

Thanks to the extraordinary people who allowed me to share in their lives while in the wilderness.

I especially thank editors, friends and mentors, Jane Self and Judy Josiah, who gave me valuable feedback on my first drafts and Pam Stanescu, Richard Goudeau and Forrest Altman for editing and fine-tuning the final manuscript. Thank you also to photographers David Aldrich and Bonnie Gehling for their great cover photographs and to John Cleaveland for his fine maps.

Heartfelt gratitude goes to Pat Blanks, Louis Lowery, Barbara Duffey, Linda Mizelle, Carolyn Flournoy, Kaye Wansley, Yvonne Elkins, Denise Lester, Dorothy Krakow, Anne Hibbard, Aubrey Hammack, Jacqui and Abrie Bester, Betty and Johan Crous and the many others who gave helpful suggestions, offered enthusiasm and gave wise counsel.

A special thank you goes to James Palmer, Editor of *The Macon Telegraph*, whose article titled *Natural Soul* and his foreword for *Earth, The Forgotten Temple* sparked the public interest in me and in the sacred, healing power of nature.

And most of all, to my husband and heart's companion, Bud Queen. Thank you for being my anchor and helping me to heal through your loving kindness.

CHAPTER 1

A SPIRITUAL BIRTH

In our tradition nature is corrupt, nature has fallen.
Joseph Campbell

Many devils are in the woods, water and wilderness, ready to hurt and prejudice people.
Martin Luther (1483-1546)

Like our European ancestors, I was afraid of facing dark forces while alone in the woods, but I would not admit it. What I talked about were the physical risks: I could break a leg, get lost and panic; I might even die. Knowing that solo camping is dangerous for a man and even more risky for a woman, I pitched my tent next to my car in parks to be near other people.

Yet friends raved about their solo wilderness treks, reporting increased awareness, deep peace and spiritual highs. Their mystical talk puzzled me but gave me hope that the jealous, vindictive God I'd heard of did not exist.

In 1978, when I was in my twenties, a friend and I backpacked a quarter-mile to Sea Camp, a campground on Georgia's Cumberland Island. Unaware that the load should be supported by the hips, I bought a cheap beltless pack and carried too much. Hanging from my out-of-shape body, the sixty-pound pack felt as if it weighed six hundred pounds. When I got to the campground's giant live oak trees with spreading limbs, I felt as if I'd hauled a truckload of bricks. Too tired to enjoy the island's miles of sparkling ocean, I swore never to backpack again. However, upon my return home, I started to jog to get in shape.

Time has a way of eroding a memory. When I was invited to backpack for a weekend in the north Georgia mountains a year later, I accepted. "I'll carry the tent, stove and food, if you tote your sleeping bag and clothes," my friend Liz volunteered. "The trail is only one-and-a-half miles, and we'll be with another couple," she added encouragingly. It seemed a generous offer, and since I had been running a mile every day, I was in better shape.

When I put on the considerably lighter beltless pack, I groaned in agony, for my shoulders started to hurt again. But it was too late. On the trail I was mesmerized by the breathtaking beauty of the towering trees and the thick oval evergreen leaves of the rhododendron forests. Our campsite, a flat grassy spot next to a bubbling brook, was magical with its cool earthy smells. The discomfort of backpacking seemed more worthwhile, but I vowed to have the proper gear in the future.

Intrigued by the enthusiasm of friends about backpacking alone, I purchased a Kelty frame pack with a padded hip belt and began making my own plans. Since it was early spring and still cool, I prepared to do my first solo hike near Juniper Springs in Florida's Ocala National Forest. The trip was a catastrophe. Picturing myself relaxing on the shore of a pristine lake, I chose a two-mile trail across slash pines to Carl's Pond. After several false starts at finding the trailhead, I asked a man in a pick-up truck for directions.

"Watch out! The trail is full of rattlesnakes," he drawled directing me to a path nearby. My apprehensions increased. Apart from occasional tall glossy green-leaved slash pine, the white sandy trail wound through a sea of knee-high fan-shaped palmetto ferns. My pace was slow. Pressed forward by my heavy pack, my eyes were mostly on the ground. By late afternoon I was still plodding in the high humidity under a brutal sun. Weary and exhausted, I trudged on. When the world dimmed into a deep shade of gold at dusk and there was no lake in sight, I reluctantly made camp on the trail near a sandy road. The two quarts of water I carried would be my only water.

Putting up my Timberline Tent was a comedy of errors. Never having put up a tent alone, I found the poles refusing to cooperate. Finally, after much effort and self pity on my part, the tent was up. Too exhausted to make dinner, I ate trail mix and drank water.

Sitting cross-legged on the sand, I glanced down and gasped. Hundreds of tiny red seed ticks were crawling up my legs. Feeling utterly miserable, I spent the evening finding the ticks with a flashlight and crushing them with my pocket knife. Luckily my tent had netting and a sewn-in floor to keep further invaders out. To ward off loneliness, I pored over my trail map, my only reading material, until deep in the night. Hoping for a visitor, I would have hugged anyone who appeared. Hurrying back to my car at first light, I drove to the nearest store to buy insect repellent and then pitched my tent in Juniper Spring's crowded campground.

In the summer of 1981, I had another invitation to backpack for three days with a friend in Georgia's Cohutta Wilderness. Remembering the beauty and peace of the mountains, I accepted. A week before we were to leave, my companion cancelled because of a crisis at work. Disappointed, I resolved to try solo backpacking again.

The night before my departure I sorted through my new purchases—light-weight Surveyor stove, summer down sleeping bag, small foam mattress, iodine pills to purify water, flashlight with extra batteries and bulb, aluminum pot, freeze dried food, powdered milk, nylon rain wear, a change of clothes and shoes, map and compass, first-aid supplies and a snake bite kit with a sharp blade and three different sized rubber suction cups. To get help or scare the bears away, I carried a whistle. My heaviest items were the seven-pound North Face Timberline tent and two one-quart plastic bottles of water. The pack weighed about thirty pounds and felt snug on my hips.

Walking tall under the towering trees and in better shape from jogging over two miles a day, I bounded down the mountain. Beads of sweat from the high humidity collected on my temples and back. The thick evergreen elliptical leaves of the mountain laurel and the bristle-tipped foliage of the oak-tree forest cast sun-dappled shadows on the babbling brook. The tiny creek slid down the mountain to join the larger Conasauga River, creating waterfalls and deep transparent pools following each other down the valley. Breathing the fresh mountain air, I felt the stress from city life dissipate like vapor. After walking a couple of miles, I set up my tent under a large red oak tree.

While sprawled wet-legged on the rocks, my mind began playing the "what if" game. What if a tree fell on me? What if someone tried to rape me? A wave of panic exploded over me like an icy sea. Sweat broke out on my temples and poured down my chest. Feeling desolate in the empty greenness, I cried like an abandoned puppy. Drowning in grief I had not allowed to surface, I sobbed for over an hour. Then it was over. Like a thunderstorm, the tears left as quickly as they came. In their place was a sense of peace; of having cast off a burden. My body felt light and carefree.

As daylight disappeared, so did my euphoria. It was so dark in my tent I could not see my hand in front of my face. My heart pounded every time I heard a snap or rustle, and the darkness magnified my terror. The mind games came back with a vengeance. I tried watching my breath ... breathing in ... breathing out, as a meditation teacher once instructed, but fear spread through my body like a fever and sapped my energy. Somehow, I drifted off to sleep.

I awoke with the warm glow of the rising sun and the soft murmur of the river. I'd made it through the night! My surroundings looked new and beautiful and I had this strange feeling of power, of being part of something much bigger than myself.

Strolling downstream to a waterfall, I sat cross-legged on a flat rock next to the whirling water. Everything fascinated me—the sparkle of light in the gurgling river, the tiny minnows darting against the current, the soft green cushion of rock moss and the strong pungent smell of the earth.

The sun slipped out from behind silver clouds filling the forest with golden shafts of light. Staring spellbound, I allowed my thoughts to turn to how I'd spent most of my thirty years taking care of day-to-day routine and not paying attention to life's bigger mysteries. To my surprise, I asked, "God, if you exist, please let me know you!" Seeking some unfathomable face, I closed my eyes. Like a heart-stopping explosion, a presence of intense love in the form of dazzling white light entered the top of my head and radiated out through my heart. The feeling was so encompassing, it was like being bathed in an ocean of ecstacy.

Bursting with bliss, I broke into violent sobs. All my life I had searched for love from others, and here it was welling up within and around me. The love was so powerful and unconditional, my heart surged with joy. Everything looked holy: the river, the trees, the plants. Looking around me with new eyes, I saw that all of creation was a sacred temple.

Feeling one with the trees, the water, the mountains, and the sky, I knew we were all of one energy and we were all connected. There was no doubt in my mind. I had experienced the presence of a God, a God that was not a big daddy in the sky but a loving energy permeating everything.

I left the mountains trembling in a state of euphoria. Now that I knew I was part of a larger field of life, time moved with new meaning. As I headed home to Macon, Georgia on the traffic-clogged interstate, I thought about my childhood.

12 Earth, the Forgotten Temple

We live on a molten planet. Rocks boil out of this creativity, we boil out of the rocks. ...To sing, the rocks became human. It is an honor that we are created out of rocks. It is something to live up to.

Brain Swimme

CHAPTER 2

CHILDHOOD YEARNINGS

At the darkest moment comes the light.
Joseph Campbell

Oceans, rivers, lakes or streams. It did not matter; I sought water as a lost fawn seeks its mother. It was true when I was a child and it is true now. I'm not sure why. Perhaps it was the roar of the Indian Ocean's giant waves crashing on the beach below my grandmother's house near Durban, South Africa. The waves lulled me to sleep at night and formed a continuous thunder during our waking hours that both calmed and stimulated awe.

Through my five-year-old eyes the sea held great mystery. She was another player in the cast of my family with moods like my grandmother. Like blue water turning savage grey, she could be peaceful, gentle and soft but at other times angry, dark and fierce. When the wind howled, the waves towered over the beach before they crashed, growling and roaring like the lions at Kruger Park.

I both loved and feared the ocean and found solace in her watery breast. She comforted a great longing for my mother, who was studying medicine in Johannesburg four hundred miles away; and for my father, whom I had never met but was told lived in America.

My mother and grandmother did not talk much about my father, but from their glances and the way they tightened their jaws, I knew they did not think well of him. My mother was eighteen when she married my father and moved to America. The marriage lasted one year. She left him and returned to South Africa shortly after my birth.

My mother's dream was to become a medical doctor, so she entered a seven-year physicians' study program in Johannesburg. When she found she was unable to study, take care of a baby, and work to support herself, my grandmother agreed to keep me.

When I was two, my grandmother sold her ocean home, and we went to live with my mother's older sister and her husband near Johannesburg. A year later, when my aunt became pregnant with her fifth child, my grandmother and I moved out. My mother, still unable to take care of me, placed me in a children's home run by nuns. I had just turned three. Six months later I hemorrhaged after a tonsillectomy and almost died.

I returned to live with my aunt whose new baby had died shortly after birth. The years with my aunt and uncle were difficult. They gave many parties, drank heavily and seemed perpetually irritated with my cousins and me.

When I turned five, my grandmother bought another house near the ocean, and I moved back in with her. My memories of the next few years were happy. Since my grandmother had retired from teaching school, she had more time to spend with me. We read books and told each other stories. When I played outside, she lay reading in a hammock that hung between two large umbrella trees or she tended her fishponds and gardens.

One day we talked about God. My grandmother said, "Niki, there is no God." I knew from the gravity in her voice she'd said something important. I shared my grandmother's beliefs with my classmates in grade school, and they pulled my hair and made fun of me. I learned to keep my mouth shut. When a friend invited me to Sunday School, I accepted out of curiosity. The solemn church atmosphere and the sermon about the fires of hell scared me. I never went back.

When my mother graduated from medical school and married my stepfather, who had just graduated from law school, I went to live with her near Johannesburg. The next few years were hard. My newly married parents were busy with each other and their new professions. I felt out of place and missed my grandmother and the ocean.

Because my parents worked long hours, I spent the day at a Catholic school but came home at night. Although I was not a Catholic, the nuns taught us about God's wrath and the torments of hell that awaited those of us who disobeyed. Not being religious, my mother did not adhere to God's rules.

"Jesus!" she yelled when angry.

"Don't say that, Mom. You'll go to hell!" I pleaded.

"That's okay; all the interesting people are there," she'd counter. Hell began to look more attractive, especially if heaven meant being stuck with the nuns without my family.

By the time I reached puberty, my mother had given birth to a daughter and a son. At thirteen, I went to a small co-ed boarding school three miles from my parents' home and stayed there for the next five years. After making new friends, I was happier. I visited my family on Sundays and holidays.

When I turned eighteen, my parents asked if I would become a South African citizen. Since I was born in the United States, I was considered an American. We were going on vacation out of the country, and I needed a passport. Because my nationality was not important to me and my being a South African seemed of value to my parents, I agreed. I attended a short naturalization ceremony and received the South African passport.

My grandmother died the year I graduated from high school. Her death took a big slice out of my heart. I spent the next three years studying art and living on the campus of a university in Johannesburg. Although I enjoyed my friends, I did not do well academically. My peers seemed so much more talented and knowledgeable. The highlight of my university years was a week-long camping trip for students on a deserted beach in Mozambique. I loved living on the seashore in a tent. Once again, the roar of the Indian Ocean became the backdrop for daily life.

When I returned to school my heart was not in my studies. I had tasted of other realms. I was now twenty-one, and my dream was to meet my father in America and wander around the globe like a gypsy. My mother helped me find my father's address in New Orleans so that I could write to him. To my surprise, he wrote back and sent me a round trip air-ticket. He had remarried but had no other children and had just retired as a ship's captain from the Merchant Marines.

I went to the American Consulate to get a visa. The Consulate looked at my South African passport and noticed I was born in New Orleans. "When did you become a South African citizen?" he asked, peering at me over his reading glasses.

"I was eighteen," I said with enthusiasm.

"You were under twenty one. You're an American," he said sternly. "You can have a American passport, not a visa!"

"My mother will kill me!" I groaned. I knew how loyal she felt about South Africa, and her dislike for America had influenced me.

"Sorry!" he said as he handed my paperwork to the clerk.

A week later I got a letter from the South African authorities. "You must relinquish your American passport immediately or you will lose your South African citizenship." The letter sounded ominous and I wondered if I should respond. I did nothing and have never regretted the decision.

I left South Africa in January 1971 in mid-summer for the winter cold of America. My newfound freedom, along with a suitcase full of clothes and four hundred dollars felt like abundance.

The meeting with my father was a big disappointment for we had little in common. I suspect I was not the quiet, adoring little girl he hoped for, and he was not the mentor I envisioned. My father, an Italian American, believed the man to be head of the household. Also, as a ship's captain he was used to having his way. At twenty-one I was trying to establish my autonomy and made the mistake of challenging his authority. After a couple of weeks we agreed it would be best if I just moved on.

While staying with my father I noticed Pan American World Airways was recruiting flight attendants in the area. Thinking that being a stewardess would be good summer work, I applied and got the job. The summer lengthened into two years.

Within a week of arriving at our base in New York City, I met Jeff Collins at a party. His talk of sailing around the world fascinated me. "Take me with you!" I pleaded.

Jeff worked as a tax lawyer on Wall Street. He was raised a Catholic in White Plains, New York. However, he broke from the church in his late teens and said he was an atheist. Since he wanted to be our sole financial support we got married shortly after I quit my two-year job with Pan Am.

For the first time I felt a sense of belonging, of being part of a family. As a teenager, Jeff had looked after his alcoholic mother. He was at home nurturing the troubled. We were a perfect match, for I was still reeling from the disappointment of meeting my father, and I had difficulty adjusting to the chaos and concrete of New York City.

Jeff became the mentor my father wasn't. He shared his books and knowledge and taught me how to cook and keep house. When Jeff got a teaching position at a law school in Macon, Georgia, he let me go back to school to get a degree in psychology. I loved my course work and felt drawn to become a children's counselor, perhaps to ease the pain from my childhood. He also taught me how to fish for bass from our aluminum canoe. Our afternoon fishing expeditions rekindled memories of the timeless magic of the great outdoors. Since I loved being outside and was less keen on fishing, he showed me how to steer the boat while he fished. When the canoe continued to go in circles, he gave up.

One summer we chartered a sailboat with four friends and hired a skipper to sail in the British Virgin Islands. This stunning ten-day experience hooked me on sailing. Jeff, however, admitted he liked the idea of sailing more than the reality.

Although Jeff had mixed feelings, he allowed me to work as a children's counselor at a clinic when I graduated. We had been married five years. Two months after I started my job, he left me for another woman, one he could take care of. My world, which had revolved around Jeff, was shattered, but he had left me with a passion for canoeing and sailing. Miraculously, I found I could paddle the canoe when we separated. Since Jeff got the boat in our divorce settlement, I purchased my own, a handsome green Mohawk.

Because I loved counseling children and their families, I stayed in Georgia to build a new life. Joining a wilderness club, I began exploring the local rivers and even learned to paddle white water. Although I enjoyed the thrill of running rapids, my real love turned out to be canoe-camping—spending the day leisurely floating down the river and camping, away from civilization, on pristine sandbars at night. I also chartered a sailboat each summer with friends to explore the Bahamas, Belize and the Florida keys.

Upon my return to Macon, I realized the effects of my encounter with God while solo backpacking were far reaching. My eyes grew wide in wonder like a child's for the world seemed fresh and new. I lost my fear of death, and since I no longer felt alone, I began to take more risks in my life, especially at work. Three of the girls I was counseling reported being molested and talked of being further traumatized by the investigation. All were told not to prosecute on the grounds of insufficient evidence—their word against an adult's was not enough. Between tears they explained how they felt they were to blame.

When I heard how other communities dealt with the situation by forming a task force and meeting regularly, I asked God to help me bring our community together. Being fearful of talking in front of large groups, I tried to reassure myself, "It won't be me: this is God's work." This was of small comfort as my faith had yet to be tested and I still had much uncertainty. Meeting with the press was equally difficult, and I found myself labeled the local "child sex abuse expert."

When I became frustrated, I reminded myself: "God is the doer. I am merely a channel." The more I learned to submit to God, the more I noticed that what I needed seemed to be provided. Believing that each person's life had a purpose and that God's Spirit worked through all of us, I decided there was no time to be self-conscious.

People also seemed different. Those who had once looked at me with indifference now looked at me with fondness. Finally, I realized it was I who had changed as deeper levels of love flowed through me. The more I got to know myself, the more compassion I had for others. Through my aloneness in the wilderness, I found my humanity. In the depth of my own story, I discovered the story of all humankind.

To understand why I had not met others who had encountered God in the wilderness, I began studying everything I could find on religion and spirituality: Christianity, Taoism, Buddhism, Hinduism and Islam. I learned I was not alone when I discovered the spirituality and traditions of the Native Americans. They talk about the Great Spirit that moves through all things. All life is sacred and part of one mother, the Earth, and one father, the Great Spirit. They believe we are given knowledge and wisdom when we are in harmony with nature. I discovered the vision quest, an ancient tradition used to connect with the Great Spirit.

A quest involves spending from one to fourteen days sitting alone in a ten-foot circle in the wilderness. No food, and in some traditions no water, is allowed. The goal is to purify the heart and body for a clear vision of our purpose on earth. In many cultures a quest is a required rite of passage to learn how to best serve the community.

After learning about the vision quest, I saw my spiritual birth in the wilderness from a new perspective. Without knowing it, I had experienced my own form of a quest and wondered what would happen if I followed more of the sacred customs. The next few years after my spiritual awakening were good. I made a new circle of friends and started to feel part of a community.

Shortly after returning from a vacation in the Bahamas I received word that my maternal aunt, with whom I had lived, had died. I was sad because I had lost touch with her. She and her husband, who was also deceased, had continued to be unhappy and drink heavily. Three months after her death, while doing a relaxation exercise, I felt her presence. Fearing her negativity, I asked her in my mind not to approach. She agreed, but to my surprise pleaded for forgiveness and prayers. My heart melted, and tears came to my eyes. Accepting her apology I sought forgiveness also. Our encounter felt like an enormous hug. Later I wondered if I'd created our meeting, but the result was healing; and I now think of her with fondness.

Feeling a need to learn more about healing and mind expansion, I began attending personal growth workshops. Three workshops in particular affected me deeply. The first course called *Silva Mind Control*, developed by Jose Silva, taught me the power of visualization. Three days of meditation and continuous visualization culminated in our creating a vivid "laboratory" in our minds with two "assistants" to help diagnose and heal people with physical or emotional problems. When the person's name, age and location were mentioned, we were told the person's image would appear on our inner visual screen and the ailments would make themselves known via visual, auditory or kinesthetic means.

Since I was skeptical, I felt sure my partner would not be able to tell what was wrong with the three people I knew with problems. I was even more sure I would not be able to accomplish such a feat. I was wrong; we all did. I learned from this that there are other realities and that we have capabilities we are not taught in our schools.

The second workshop to have a profound effect on me was a five-day *Living, Dying and Transition* workshop given by Elizabeth Kubler-Ross. Elizabeth believes that each of us has the capacity to love others unconditionally and that it is our unfinished business that keeps us from doing so. In her workshop she created an environment in which we were encouraged to express our hurt and rage in an atmosphere of love and acceptance, so we could be done with them.

Feelings were not to be talked about but felt. If sad, we cried; if angry, we were given a rubber hose and an old telephone book and were told, "Have at it!" Again I was skeptical about what this outpouring of negativity would accomplish. Yet it worked, and I was amazed as depressed or hostile people transformed themselves into radiant, loving persons right before my eyes. I realized in this workshop that we are all connected and that our life stories are much the same.

The third workshop was titled *The Firewalk: Turning Fear Into Power* by Anthony Robbins. Again, I could not believe that two hundred people, myself included, could walk on hot coals and not get burned. I suspected a hoax, a fast walk on coals that had cooled, or wet feet. Instead we were instructed to walk the length of fifteen feet of coals at a slow, even pace. The heat from the coals forced us to stand at some distance, and we only wet our feet afterwards. What was the trick? The "trick" had to do with faith and with learning to turn fear into power. These workshops helped me see that we create our own realities, that fear limits us from fully realizing our potentials and that we all have capabilities far beyond our knowledge.

22 Earth, the Forgotten Temple

Seven years after my divorce from Jeff, I bought a house on a lake and remarried. My husband, John Nakles, moved into my home, but I soon found myself in the role of caretaker. Although we shared similar spiritual beliefs, I became so absorbed in John's problems I had no life of my own. Within two years I was divorced again.

Here I was, thirty-nine and alone. It felt natural to turn to the wilderness, especially the water, to heal and to do a spiritual quest. Tradition calls for a guide when doing a vision quest, but I could not find one. Although I was apprehensive about the fast, I wanted to do a quest so badly that I made my own plans over the next few months. Since water is important to me, I decided to do a spirit quest (my version of a vision quest) on a river bank.

Georgia has an abundance of creeks and rivers flowing through the state like blood through our veins. My choices were many: clear mountain streams in the north, wide silent rivers in the south or the ocean along Georgia's marshy coast. It felt right to do my first spirit quest on the two hundred and fifty-mile long Suwannee River, with its many isolated white sandbars in Georgia and Florida.

The Suwannee River's name comes from the Indian word *sawni* meaning "echo." Stephen Foster immortalized the river when he wrote, "Way Down Upon the Swanee River" in the 1850s.

The Suwannee River and the Okefenokee Swamp were under the ocean during Pleistocene times. As the ocean receded, and today's shoreline was established, a body of shallow water was caught in a depression and became a fresh water lake. The lake drained southwest into the Gulf of Mexico forming the Suwannee River and into the Atlantic in the southeast forming the St. Mary's River. A pamphlet distributed by the Georgia State Parks said, "The story of the origin and development of the Okefenokee Swamp and the Suwannee River has been half a million years, perhaps longer, in the writing, and it is not yet finished."

Doc Billingslea, a friend, heard I was going to spend two weeks canoeing down the Suwannee River and asked if he could join me. Since he was willing to bring his own canoe so we could separate when I began my spirit quest, I agreed.

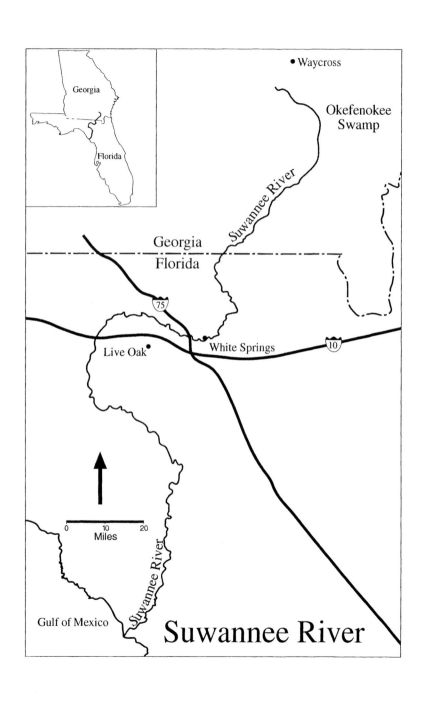

Waycross

Okefenokee
Swamp

Suwannee River

Georgia
Florida

75

Live Oak

White Springs

10

Miles
0   10   20

Suwannee River

Gulf of Mexico

Suwannee River

CHAPTER 3

THE SUWANNEE RIVER

Revelation comes in two volumes——the Bible and nature.
Thomas Aquinas

I'd known Doc a year and was intrigued by his life-style. He had stopped teaching high school chemistry in his mid-thirties and had not been employed for twenty years. He called himself a "river rat" and spent most of his time canoeing and hiking. Although he was not wealthy, he lived simply off the interest from his savings.

Doc and I started our odyssey in the summer of 1989 from Griffis Fish Camp, located just south of the Okefenokee swamp about seventeen miles north of Fargo, Georgia, the nearest town. We left our cars at the camp owner's house, and he agreed to pick us up in Doc's van two weeks later.

Once we were on the river, dark cool shadows of low white clouds skittered across the water and sheltered us from the blazing sun. The black water, low from lack of rain, ran between two white sandy shores. Green oval-leafed tupelo trees lined the banks, their thick trunks and serpentine roots entwining like the limbs of lovers. Tall slender broad-based cypress trees with green needle-like leaves looked elegant next to the squatty gnarled tupelo. Silver-gray streams of Spanish moss hung on their branches like tinsel on Christmas trees. The Spanish moss is a series of tiny interlaced plantlets without roots that feed on airborne nutrients in moisture.

The Suwannee emerges from the Okefenokee Swamp in south Georgia and meanders in a southwesterly direction through Florida. It cuts through Florida's sand hills and limestone cliffs before it widens into a large coastal swamp. The Suwannee's rich tea color comes from tannic acid, created when acidic water mixes with peat. The river is also fed by a number of large deep limestone aquifers that bubble up as fresh water springs, so clear that weeds and fish can be seen twenty feet below the surface.

In June 1980, the State of Florida Environmental Regulation Commission designated the Suwannee an "Outstanding Florida Water." This act prohibits further degradation of the river through pollution. Unfortunately, Georgia has been less vigilant about protecting its natural resources. In early 1997, Dupont owned and wanted to mine the white pigment called titanium dioxide on a three by thirty mile stretch of land on the eastern border of the Okefenokee Refuge, which affects the Suwannee. Alarmed by the outbursts of resistance, Dupont has temporarily halted its plans.

Doc paddled his red Blue Hole canoe with two fierce-looking white and black dragons painted on the sides while I was in my ten-year-old Mohawk. His stroke was rhythmic, almost leisurely. At times he looked like a young boy with clear blue eyes, but at other times he seemed more his age, a man in his late fifties with thinning gray hair. He was smiling, but occasionally his smile appeared more like a grimace. Doc's clothes reminded me of a flower gone to seed. His olive green shirt and khaki shorts looked threadbare and stained, and hung on his slender brown body like limp petals. His clothes smelled faintly of mold.

Doc told me about Amy, his new girlfriend. "She looks like a model, with long black hair and blue eyes. She's really beautiful," he said dreamily. "And she's rich; you should see her jewelry!" he laughed. "Once she lost a diamond earring in the van ... it cost more than the van!"

"Did you find it?"

"We had to!" he sighed. "You should have seen us tear the van apart."

"How does she feel about your canoeing with me for two weeks?"

Doc picked up his paddling pace. "Well," he said slowly, "She thinks I'm canoeing with David." He peeked at me and chuckled, his eyes shifting from side to side.

"You lied to her!"

"Yeah ... well ... she wouldn't understand ... you know." His smile appeared frozen.

"Honesty is best," I sighed.

"All is illusion," Doc shot back.

I stared at him in disbelief. "Even if the universe is an illusion, the challenge is to walk in truth!" Doc's face twitched with an amused expression. I changed the subject.

"You'll be camping a mile or two downstream when I do my spiritual quest. Would you mind checking on me?" I inquired nervously. "I've never done a fast before."

"That's fine," he said indulgently. "Hope you don't pass out or something!"

When the cypress tree shadows lengthened to form zebra stripes across the black water, we found a campsite. It was a large white pristine-looking sandbar surrounded by cypress trees and dense thickets of dark evergreen fan-shaped palmetto ferns.

We set up our tents, and then collapsed in the shallow black water to cool off. Facing upstream, we dug our hands into the sandy bottom and floated gently in the current like seaweed in a tidal pool. The vibrating water washed over us, replacing our seared emotions with utter peace. Towering cumulus thunderheads to the west gave off a deep rumble, but the sky above us remained clear. Refreshed, we sat on a plastic tarp and shared a dinner of precooked hamburger, salad and fresh pineapple.

I pulled a dead Monarch butterfly with orange and black ringed wings towards me to admire its velvet veneer. When I looked again, large black ants were carrying it off. Doc noticed them too, and we sat quietly to watch. Most Monarch butterflies survive. Navigating by the sun, they fly over two thousand miles to winter in central Mexico or California.

Once there, they hang like fur on coniferous trees that they've used for generations. During the journey the year-old females lay their eggs which hatch into caterpillars before turning into butterflies to fly north.

"Ouch!" Doc jumped up and yelled while swatting his feet. "Fire ants." We quickly rose, brushed ourselves off and moved the tarp to fresh ground. Related to wasps, these tiny red ants inject painful formic acid. Big-headed horseflies with iridescent wings had also made large hurtful incisions when feeding on our blood. In pain, we squashed them with a sharp slap.

Only a few mosquitoes appeared at sunset. We thought the drought might have dried up the water that their larvae needed to survive. A delicately built female mosquito with a single pair of wings and long fragile legs used her elongated proboscis on my hand to suck blood for food. I idly brushed her off.

Since it was too hot to build a fire, we went to bed. My tent was warm even without the rain fly, which keeps the tent dry but blocks some of the air circulation. I envied Doc with his tent of netting and thought how it had to be a whole lot cooler. Sleep would not come.

A barred owl chortled what sounded like "Who cooks for you?" Its mate answered in soft mysterious throaty murmurs. Finally, a breeze cooled the air, and I fell asleep. When I woke up, the sun, a large red glowing ball, was just above the horizon, and the air was cool.

My mind was in a fog when we started down the river. Irritated by a biting fly that left painful bleeding wounds, I paddled hard and moved ahead. The water flowed slowly, its dark black surface mirroring the green tupelo leaves. Two iridescent jewel-colored blue damselflies and a larger gray dragonfly hitched a ride on my dry bags. The dragonfly took off like a torpedo and made a series of long skimming flights across the water. I'm told dragonflies can reach a speed of up to thirty miles per hour. Another graceful blue damselfly landed on a clump of green reeds along the shore. Gazing spellbound, I stopped to watch. Arching its long slender abdomen, it placed its tail in the water, perhaps to deposit some eggs. Pulsing and gliding, it took to the air and disappeared. Wanting to share what I had seen, I thought about waiting for Doc, but the image of relaxing on a quiet pretty sandbar made me paddle harder.

The dark scaly head of a small alligator glided through the water about ten feet ahead of me. I tightened my grip on the canoe paddle and stopped as if turned to stone. The raised dark V of its bow-wave sent a circle of ripples around its head. It turned slowly to stare with brown glassy eyes, then moved to the left bank, hissed explosively and walloped the water with its tail. The waves crashed and whipped the air. Jerking backwards, I squinted at its snake-like eyes. The ripples rolled to the bank and flattened.

Doc appeared downstream. Raising my hand in warning, I pointed. When he came abreast, he silently handed me his camera, but it was too late. The alligator slowly sank among silver bubbles behind a stack of logs.

I learned later that alligators are close relatives of the dinosaur. Although they average eight to ten feet in length, a few grow up to nineteen feet. The female builds a nest of vegetation and lays thirty to sixty eggs in the spring. The rotting vegetation incubates the eggs, and when they hatch in two months, the eight-inch striped baby 'gators signal the mother to open the nest via grunting noises. Formerly hunted for their skins, they have been protected by State and Federal laws since the 1960s and are very important in the balance of nature. The holes they make in the water for protection against cold and drought also provide habitats for fish and other species during low water.

Doc dropped behind while I paddled under the shady trees to stay cool. A great blue heron stood statuesquely waiting for fish in an inlet. I paused to watch. It waited patiently for a couple of minutes, then stabbed a minnow with its beak. The heron swallowed the fish's silvery head first so the spines on its fins pointed backwards and did not snag on the bird's throat. With wings making a slow rowing action in the air, it flew downstream and landed on the water. Floating like a goose it disappeared in the reeds.

I was surprised to learn that herons live in large colonies and build their nests in trees where they take turns with their mates sitting on their eggs for twenty-eight days. Herons from the south do not migrate to Central or South America like those that live up north.

The canoe suddenly stopped, grounded on a sandbar. It felt good to do heavy physical labor hauling the boat over the sandy bottom and to sweat in the sweltering heat. Then I lay in the water to cool off.

When the sun was so high I could no longer find shade, I stopped on a sandy spit under two large tupelo trees. Twenty minutes later Doc joined me for lunch. Lounging on a small lawn chair in the cool river, I began to relax. Doc also underwent a metamorphosis. When he had arrived he looked old and sad with cloudy gray eyes. Now after an hour of being gently caressed by the water, he looked years younger and his eyes were blue and clear. "Doc, you look happy!" I said laughing.

"So do you!"

When the tree shadows lengthened, we searched for a larger sandbar for the night. It felt pleasant to paddle in silence, together but separate. As the sun sank low on a red horizon, we found a large white sandbar.

"You can share my tent if you like," Doc suggested. "It's cooler than yours." I accepted gratefully. While I set up the tent, he fried two steaks for dinner. Dark thunderclouds gathered and it began to sprinkle. Doc pulled out a small umbrella to keep us dry. For our last luxury meal we feasted on the steaks, fresh pineapple and ice cold lemonade. The clearing sky, framed by black tree silhouettes, turned beautiful shades of pink. Slowing down, we felt content.

With darkness, billions of brilliant stars silently exploded into view.

"Do you mind if I start my spirit quest tomorrow?" I inquired looking up at the heavens.

"It's okay with me," Doc's voice echoed through the dark.

"I think I'll do a two-day rather than a three-day quest," I said feeling apprehensive.

"Two nights?" he clarified, sounding relieved. The stars shimmered like diamonds through the tent net. A breeze cooled the air.

At sunrise I awoke feeling refreshed. Somewhere in the distance I heard machinery. Was it a bulldozer or a chain saw? Resenting the noise, I wondered if I should postpone my quest. "No, no excuses. I'm going through with this," I told myself firmly.

We found a place downstream behind a tree to build a small stick tepee so Doc could check on me after the first night. If he saw my tepee, it would mean I was safe and there was no need to disturb me. The river glinted silver in the sun when we hugged good-bye.

> Every ripple and eddy of this lovely stream seemed solemnly
> to feel the presence of the Creator.
>
> John Muir

CHAPTER **4**

THE SPIRIT QUEST

How do you approach the biblical wisdom, the holy wisdom of creatures?
You approach it with silence. You need a silent heart to listen to the
wisdom of the wind and the wisdom of the trees and the wisdom of the
waters and soil....The second coming of Christ will not be the bodily
return of Christ, but a dawning consciousness of the divinity of the planet
and all things.

Matthew Fox

Books on vision quests recommend sitting in a ten-foot
circle, but my site was less formal. It was a sandy area next
to the river surrounded by seven small tupelo trees. The
tupelos provided shade and there seemed to be fewer fire
ants.

A cool breeze softly touched my skin as I sat naked on
my mat. Being alone without clothes made me feel closer to
Great Spirit—more exposed, natural, and innocent like a
child. Caressed by the sun, wind and air, my skin and senses
tingled with aliveness.

I wondered if I would hear voices or soar in ecstatic
reverie. Closing my eyes I prayed. "Help me to know you,
Great Spirit. Help me to heal and be a clear channel for your
work." The tears that flowed made me feel open and
vulnerable.

Thoughts of the many great spiritual teachers who have
quested came to mind. Christ went into the wilderness for
forty days and nights to fast and pray before he began His
ministry. Buddha spent six years alone in the forest and later
with a band of ascetics, practicing self-control and self-denial
before his enlightenment under a fig tree. He then went back
into the world to teach for forty-five years. Mohammed spent
fifteen years meditating in a cave, sometimes all night, before
he heard the voice of Allah and wrote the Koran, the Moslem

Bible. His writing was a miracle since he had never gone to school and could barely write his name.

At least a hundred metallic green whirligig beetles darted back and forth on the water's surface. Their oval hard backs moved in unison with the leader and their long front legs created a tiny dimple on the water's film. A scaly golden brown lizard with blue patches on its throat and legs scurried up a tree when a robust hairy-looking yellow and black bumble-bee settled on my mat and started to clean its legs.

As time crept by I wondered if I could fast for two days. Hours had passed since I started my quest, and the hunger was becoming harder. Calling to the Great Spirit again and again I asked, "What is my purpose on earth? How can I best serve my brothers and sisters? How can I help heal the earth?" Then I listened in silence. To still my thoughts I watched my breath ... breathing in ... breathing out, but my mind rebelled, and I thought about work. Was counseling my life's purpose? Like a butterfly, my mind fluttered from one thought to the next.

A small yellow bird swooped across the river and landed on the lizard's tree. It chirped a couple of times before it flitted upstream. Two black buzzards circled effortlessly below a tall white cloud, their wide outstretched wings catching a thermal. Their tails broadened and narrowed as they spiralled upwards in a column of invisible rising air. Something tickled my toe. Looking down I was surprised to see a fire ant scurrying across my foot. Why did it not bite?

Wisps of white billowy clouds drifted eastward as the sun swung higher on the sky's blue dome. Lying wet-legged on a mat watching small round ripples form on the water from a puff of wind, I realized I was not lonely. My senses had come alive, and I felt rich.

In a heartbeat my serenity was gone. The river and trees did not look so friendly, and my head ached with a dull pain. Going without food for twenty hours made me feel as if I were waiting to die and didn't care. The thought of last night's steak was torture.

Seeking the moisture in my eyes, little white gnats with tiny feet tickled my face. I gently brushed them away. My mouth went dry. A vision of an alligator tearing at the flesh of my thigh with its sharp teeth stuck in my mind. It could silently drag and hold me at the bottom of the river till I drowned. The harder I tried to ignore the picture, the more it clung to my thoughts like a briar. Remembering I had no weapon, I spied the canoe paddle.

For shame! Where did such thoughts come from? I came into the woods with love in my heart, even for the alligators. No, I would carry no weapon and suffer the consequences; passive resistance, Ghandi style. Tears flowed for my good intentions. I called to the Great Spirit, "Please Mother-Father God, Great Spirit, purify me, help me to heal." Praying helped; my mind began to clear.

The air seemed cooler. I squinted at the sun, hoping more time had passed, but the sun was high above the horizon. Disappointed, I looked at the trees and drew strength from their grounded solidness. I must have fallen asleep for when I woke I felt much better.

The setting sun looked like an orange ball peeking through the trees. Fasting was humbling—I felt more fragile but also more vulnerable and open.

When I squatted to tinkle, fresh raccoon tracks, two adults and a youngster, were visible in the sand next to me. Since raccoons give birth to an average of four young, I wondered what had happened to the other offspring. To my dismay, large black ants congregated around my urine, when I left.

My bed, a sheet on top of a sleeping bag with a plastic mat underneath, was ready. This was my first time sleeping outside a tent, and I was nervous. Except for a bird singing in the distance, all was quiet. A few mosquitoes hovered around me, but my body was protected by my sleeping bag, and my face by a small mesh dome. The rushing river and the wheeling stars shimmered in the dark.

When I called out to the Great Spirit, tears welled up from deep within. "Help me to let go of my ego and the physical world and to know my spirit." A soft breeze appeared from nowhere. Realizing how blessed I was in my life, and that Doc was nearby and would check on me, my mind became still. Sleep finally came. The next morning I felt hungry and haggard.

The reeds on the opposite bank swayed with a gentle breeze, alternately showing their leaf-sheathed stems and their crested yellow tops. They looked like an ever-changing sea of green and gold. When the breeze stopped there was only the voice of the water murmuring as it worked its way between the shores. Without the usual busy work, I found I was paying more attention to my surroundings.

The river looked peaceful in the morning sun. It was hard to tell the real bank from its mirror image. When horse flies appeared, I asked them to please not bite me in this sacred circle. It seemed to work for awhile, but they returned when I moved around.

"Bang," came the sound of an oar hitting the side of the canoe down river.

"Oh no, I've not built the tepee!" I groaned peeking from behind the trees. Sure enough, Doc was slowly paddling upstream, grinning broadly.

"Hello," I called; slipping on a shirt. "You're early."

"It only took me half an hour to get up here."

"You found a sandbar okay?"

"Yes, it's nice! Just wanted to check to see you had not passed out," he said slowly turning his canoe around.

"Thanks," I yelled. "This is hard," I thought. "What a way to spend a vacation!"

Sometimes the river's surface looked like glass; at other times there were ripples from a downstream breeze. The water's moods changed like mine.

My hunger from almost thirty-one hours of fasting was more bearable when I sat in the water. One by one tiny silver minnows flashed in the shallows, but scattered and gathered when I moved around. I cupped my hands in front of them and held my breath. To my utter amazement about a half dozen darted in. To test their trust I whisked my fish-filled hands in the air and released them with a splash. They returned when I cupped my hands again. Time elapsed while I provided the fish with a fun-filled waterfall.

Feeling wild-eyed, I stretched and returned to my mat. The small squat body of a spotted gray frog jumped in front of me. It was so well camouflaged, I hardly saw it. Hopping across the sandbar with its powerful hind legs and webbed feet, it stopped to rest every four or five leaps. I was fascinated to learn that males call their mates by using an inflated balloon-like sac as a resounding chamber while females are usually voiceless except for cries of alarm. Before the coming of songbirds millions of years ago, the call of frogs and toads was the earth's most musical sound.

During the night I awoke to see two stars streak across the sky. "Falling stars," I whispered and made a wish. When I opened my eyes in the morning a big hairy spider sat on the inside of my net. I nervously chased it out with my hands. I called to the Great Spirit for guidance. Nothing came back, no emotion, no good feelings. Had I lost contact?

A spirit quest is a hero's journey—the confrontation of our inner demons. Do I slay or befriend the dragons of my mind, the stream of trivial thoughts that keeps me from communing with Great Spirit? Repeating a chant I'd heard on tape, "Oh Great Spirit, Earth, Sun, Sky and Sea. You're inside and all around me," lifted my spirits. So far my fast had made me feel both heavy and light, weak and strong, full and empty, disoriented and in harmony.

An owl cooed upstream. Having heard that owls call our name when we die, I hoped it was not warning me about death—not yet anyway. Perhaps it was a summons for an ego death and a rebirth in spirit.

On the river my body felt alive, my senses keen. Without having the chores of preparing, eating and cleaning up of meals, life had become simpler. It did not matter if I were male or female, what I did for a living, where I came from, what I wore or who my family and friends were. My nationality, income and possessions did not mean anything here. I sat with nothing, doing nothing—and I felt rich. A fish jumped clear out of the water and returned with a "plop." It startled me.

When the sun, low in the sky, cast the world in a yellow light, I thought about my first encounter with Great Spirit— that incredible love welling up within and around me. Coming from a family of atheists, I had not thought much about God. One life seemed easy, for there was oblivion at the end. My spiritual birth changed that, for I now know Great Spirit flows through us into eternity. We are accountable for the earth, the people, the animals, the plants—for the planet's survival.

A shiver went up my spine. The painful memory of the last visit with my mother surfaced. We had fought and now four years later my letters remained unanswered. Looking up at the whirling darkness, I cried, "Great Spirit, if you are loving, why is there suffering in the world?" Embraced by a calm, I closed my eyes and swayed in silence.

Suddenly, I was kneeling on brown cobblestones among a mob of shouting people in gray robes. Before us, a man who radiated peace staggered bare-footed under a heavy wooden cross. Pieces of his ragged purple robe fell from his frame as he stumbled up the road that uncoiled like a cobra. The throng cried, "Away with Jesus of Nazareth; crucify him!" A crown of thorns pierced his head, and blood trickled into his kind-looking eyes. A sob caught in my throat. He swayed and dropped to the earth. I crumbled and blacked out.

Boom! Boom! a great hammering echoed across the valley when I came to. My heart skipped. They were nailing him to the cross. Crouching where I had fallen, I wailed, "Why? Why?"

Back on the river the words, *Why not!* exploded into my consciousness. Astonished and trembling, I sat up and opened my eyes. From deep within I heard, *Like each of you, Jesus had to be betrayed and crucified. How else can you learn unconditional love?* My problem suddenly seemed minuscule compared to Jesus.' If this beautiful man could accept and forgive those that had slain Him, I could too.

The silver river shimmered in the dark. Transfigured, I felt huge and luminous. More revelations coursed through my mind: *Evil is but another mask of God and is required to master unconditional love. Opposites such as good and evil are necessary to learn to forgive. Loss teaches us to let go of the material world and our planet is only one learning place in the universe.*

Tears of awe flowed like the black silent stream. Great Spirit and all creation were of one energy and larger and more powerful than I had ever imagined. I peered into the darkness with new eyes; the river became not just a river— but a universe. All of creation glowed within me. Awakened by the glimpse of God's vastness, I vowed to be less fearful on my earth walk. This bright, wild, dangerous world had become God's gift. Content, I fell asleep. During the night I woke and looked at the stars—bright points of light on a dark moonless dome. Great Spirit had blessed me, but I felt that the rest of the journey would provide more understanding and that my capacity to forgive would be tested in the future.

40 Earth, the Forgotten Temple

Woe unto them that join house to house, that lay field to field, till there be no place, that they may be placed alone in the midst of the earth.
Isaiah 4:8

CHAPTER 5

REUNION

The ultimate aim of the quest must be neither release nor ecstasy for oneself, but the wisdom and the power to serve others.

Joseph Campbell

I opened my eyes. The sun shot out from a silver cloud and streams of sunlight poured through the trees. The air was still and cool. Dazed and slightly nauseated, I ate two oranges to break my fast. They tasted very sweet, and energy replaced the nausea. The morning sun slanted across the beach and shone in my eyes when I broke camp.

Paddling slowly to Doc's campsite I wondered if my vision had been a dream? It had felt very real. Trembling with excitement, I resolved to keep it to myself. The knowledge was new, and I needed time to absorb it. Whirling eddies welled up where my paddle hit, the ripples fanning downstream. Everything on earth seemed holy.

A white egret with a yellow bill stood motionless in the reeds. It let me get within a couple of feet before it flew downstream. Feeling in rhythm with the lazy river, I paddled quietly, hoping to sneak up on Doc. I was almost there.

"Squawk ... squawk!" Another white egret sounded the alarm. "No!" I muttered. Doc's smiling face peered at his tent door.

"Hi," he waved.

Beaching my canoe, I walked over. "I tried to be silent, but an egret gave me away."

"Yeah. I have friends, you know!" he said with a laugh. We hugged. "How was your solo?" I asked inquisitively.

"Great; I even did a semi-fast. How about you?"

"It was an ordeal, but wonderful!" We exchanged stories while Doc took down his tent. My first "big" meal of cold canned vegetables and chicken soup tasted incredible.

42 Earth, the Forgotten Temple

The river looked dark and mysterious in the morning sun. To protect my skin from the sun while canoeing, I wore a white long-sleeved shirt, long white pants and a white curtained peak cap. Doc said they made me look like a rich Arab.

We paddled slowly with Doc a short distance behind me. A doe ambled with easy stride towards the water downstream. Her walk was firm and confident, not the least suspicious of danger. The tips of her soft brown hair caught in the sunlight and shone like polished gold. I motioned to Doc to look, but the doe froze, then bounded off with her white tail in the air. We gaped when she made a glorious leap over a hedge of shoulder-high palmettoes and vanished.

Doc stopped to take pictures of a huge live-oak tree that hung over the water's edge creating a cool cave under its gigantic green dome. Continuing on around a bend, I looked ahead and gasped. A large, golden brown, cat-like animal half-crouched to drink water. Its head, body and tail were in a dead line. Except for the small round head and flattened ears, it looked like a young African lioness. Staring spellbound, I stopped paddling. The silence was absolute. With eyes fixed unblinkingly on me, she turned and raised her head, then with a flick of her tail she bolted off into the bush. Blinking in disbelief, I continued to sit.

Thinking it might be a Florida panther, I remembered with sadness how they once ranged from eastern Texas through to the Southeastern United States but are now on the federal endangered species list. Hunting at night for deer, wild pigs and rabbits, they can cover from twenty to thirty miles. Being territorial, they use scent markers to identify their territory.

When Doc caught up with me, I exploded with excitement about the panther. We had just pitched the tent at the next sandbar when dark clouds rolled in. A bolt of lightning lit the sky, followed by a deafening thunder clap. It began to rain very hard. Taking refuge in Doc's tent, we talked about the panther, then drifted into idle chatter about other people. "Let's stay in the present," I asked wistfully.

"Be here now!" Doc grinned.

It was hot and humid when the rains stopped. We had dinner and strolled down the beach. When we turned in, the sky cleared and the stars twinkled through the tent's mesh dome. A chorus of crickets and the high metallic trill of frogs filled the night air. "I'd like to make a tape of the night sounds sometime," Doc said with enthusiasm.

"Yeah, they put me in a trance," I said sleepily. We could also hear the distant sounds of a car engine and a dog barking.

Gray clouds clogged the sky at daybreak. The forecast on the weather radio called for a sixty percent chance of thunderstorms, but it looked as if the clouds were about to burn off.

A loud splash came from upstream; looking around I was surprised to see Doc half swimming, half walking in the middle of the river. We packed the canoes and headed for Fargo, the last of civilization for awhile. Two hours later, we were still paddling. The sun got hotter but still no Fargo.

"Paddle over here!" Doc yelled. "Stop right there, that's the picture I want," he said pointing to a big cypress tree with a hole in the middle.

"Yes ... sir!" I shouted trying to hold still. "I've known you a year and I've yet to see one of your pictures," I teased. "I don't think you develop them!"

Doc laughed, "Yeah, I don't have any film in the camera."

We finally passed Fargo, and the further I got from it, the more peaceful I felt. I paddled in front. Doc said he liked it that way.

A white-tailed doe stood facing the water's edge. She slowly turned her head and her soft brown eyes regarded me with mild curiosity. I beached my canoe on a log and we gazed at each other. Then with a warning whisk of her white tail she gave a sneezy snort and cantered off into the woods. Sparks of her soul seemed to stay with me.

Although a healthy doe gives birth to twins each year, white tailed deer were exterminated in Georgia earlier this century. They were later reintroduced from out of state and have become abundant due to scientific wild life management.

We stopped at a sand bar for lunch. Doc's face looked drawn and pinched. "I can't stop thinking about my dog," he said mournfully. "He's dying!" His face paled as tears welled up. He looked up and smiled through his tears. He said his ex-wife was taking care of their twelve-year-old boxer. I felt sad for him.

Later in the afternoon dark angry-looking storm clouds gathered from the north. We set up camp on a snow-white sandbar near three tall old cypress trees enclasped by ferns and lichen. The tent was just up when it began to pour. Doc crawled inside. "I want to be out in the rain," I told Doc. He grinned before zipping up the tent.

Mother Earth's watery, windy hands messaged my body while I stood waist deep in the warm water. Black waves lapped against the twisted roots of the trees and the white sandy shore. The rain drops tickled my shoulders and face when I glided across the river. The river water jumped up to meet the beating rain, creating tiny water spouts and small translucent bubbles. "Crack!" came the sound of thunder seconds after a flash of lightning. A small round circle of light formed where the clouds broke. It felt good to be alive.

"Doc, come join me," I yelled in delight. There was a sound of the tent zipper before a smiling face appeared at the tent entrance. When the rain stopped, we had dinner in the hot, steamy air.

Four anhingas circled our site and settled on the top of the cypress trees. Lying back, we admired their sinuous shiny black bodies, long elegant necks and heads with pointed bills for catching fish and insects. With heads raised, the anhingas made deep throaty sounds like an echo in a hollow chamber. Since their less porous feathers absorb water, I'd often spied them sitting in the sun, with a spread-wing pose to dry their wings. I'd also seen them swimming with their snake-like heads and necks above water when not diving.

All was quiet until we brought out the binoculars. Like a bomb explosion, they took off flapping in every direction. "Sorry, birds, I didn't mean to disturb you," I apologized.

When it started to rain again, Doc got in the tent. I sat under the umbrella to watch the lights dim as dusk set in. The anhingas returned and settled in the cypress tree behind our camp. They were quiet except for an occasional squawk when we giggled. We felt honored by their presence.

That night I dreamed about a radiant East Indian spiritual teacher. Some friends and I were sponsoring a workshop for her at the beach. The teacher and I had a wonderful, loving, wordless energy exchange in the conference room. But instead of attending her workshop, I went to the beach to be with the water spirits. My teacher had become nature, and leaving the ocean seemed unthinkable.

We awoke to an overcast sky, but the sun peeked out while we were having breakfast. Our night companions, the anhingas, had long since flown away. After a long cool swim I emerged from the water. "You look like a goddess," Doc said admiringly.

Just as we were about to leave, a small brown and orange water snake with yellow stripes came to visit between our canoes. With the grace of a ballet dancer, its little body turned right, then left. Pivoting on its axis, it swam off. Since the snake is a symbol of transmutation it seemed like a good omen!

Our paddling was silent. The animals would have to see or smell us from then on. Hardy cypress trees stood in the noisy fast-flowing current of Swanoochie Creek at our next stop. The creek entering the Suwannee behind our sandbar was surrounded by an old cypress forest with many short round-tipped bark-covered cypress knees.

The shrill cry of a red-tailed hawk pierced the air. It gave off two more cries, then it crossed the river and circled us. My heart leapt with delight. Gazing at the hawk, I thought how our ancestors believed hawks to be God's messengers heralding an important event.

After lunch Doc lay on the mat to take a nap. I sat hypnotized by the dancing, flickering sparkle on the water's surface. Noticing movement to my left, I turned my head and gasped. Within a few feet of me, a doe stepped daintily towards the river on her long delicate legs. Looking slowly around, she gave me a long, full gaze with her soft brown eyes then gently lowered her snout and ambled past. Doc sat up when I touched his shoulder. The scene seemed like a fairyland in which some spell held us. The doe, unfrightened, waded into the water and glided across the river. When she emerged on the far bank her golden brown body shone in the sunlight. Facing away, she cupped her large oval ears forward and sniffed the air. With easy confidence she gazed back, seeming to say good-bye, and strolled behind a thicket of tupelo trees. Watching in speechless ecstasy, I wept.

There is something sacred and eternal about a deer's presence, a purity of spirit that touches the heart and takes me back to my first encounter with Great Spirit. It came as no surprise when I later learned that deer are a symbol of love for the Huichol Indians in Mexico.

Doc and I followed the deer's fresh tracks to a small sandy hill. We could tell from her many footprints that she had stood there a long time. Stirred by our encounter with the doe, we decided to spend the night.

Dark clouds gathered from the west, threatening another thunderstorm. Doc paddled his canoe farther down the sandbar to set up the tent. I ambled over. The sun was still shining when a gentle rain began. We sat under the umbrella until it started to pour. Doc disappeared inside the tent.

Staring unblinkingly at the raindrops that jumped, flickered and fell, I pictured the many animals that are now extinct which once populated the Suwannee river. The Eastern Bison was last seen in Florida around 1800. The Passenger Pigeon, believed to be the most numerous bird which ever existed, was last seen in Florida in 1893. The Parakeet, Bachman's Warbler, American Ivory-Billed Woodpecker and the Dusty Seaside Sparrow all were killed off by hunters at the turn of the century. The last Florida black bear was killed in 1908. How I would have loved to see these animals. Extinction is forever, I pondered sorrowfully.

Four large black birds with white heads, black wings and black slightly forked tails circled our camp and settled in a dead cypress tree across the river. They squawked and preened in the rain, creating an air of excitement and festivity. I got the binoculars to take a closer look. "Hey, Doc ... come and look at these birds!" Doc studied the birds through the binoculars from the tent doorway.

"Wow, they look like falcons with swallow-shaped tails!" I later learned they were swallow-tailed kites.

My river bath felt warm in the cold drizzle. The sprinkle stopped, and Doc ambled over to join me. "I bet alligators accidentally pass us in the water and think, 'Whew! That was close.'" I said smiling. Doc chuckled.

"Have you noticed we're not being bitten by fire ants?" he asked thoughtfully.

"I know, and I'm puzzled." After dinner we watched the world grow dim. "My spirit quest felt like a purification for the rest of the journey," I said softly.

"Oh?"

"Never have I felt so alive, so rich, so blessed. One peak experience follows the next," I said blinking back tears.

Doc's smile broadened. "Yeah, I know what you mean." Clouds blocked the stars when a barred owl chortled a haunting hoot, its throaty chuckle echoing through the night.

48 Earth, the Forgotten Temple

The next morning our falcon friends were squawking and seemed to expect some kind of entertainment. They were lined up facing us. I shook out Doc's ground cloth. The birds took to the air screeching and hovered, kicking up a ruckus. "You're laughing at your earth-bound relatives," I chuckled.

When it got hot on the river, we paddled in the shade under the trees. A beaver the size of a cat approached my canoe. Its smooth V-shaped wake spread out from its furry pear-shaped head. Astonished, I stopped paddling and held my breath. It circled my canoe with its coal black nose turned up in the water. We gazed at each other, then "ka-sploosh, splash," it walloped the water's surface with its spoon-shaped tail and dove deep into the river.

"Did you see that?" I said stunned. Doc nodded and grinned. Staring at the silver bubbles that rose where the beaver had left, I thought how our ancestors regarded the beaver as a symbol of cooperation and industry. Building a shelter with its partner by piling logs and sticks across woodland streams, it has a strong sense of family and home.

I had fond memories of hearing beavers gnawing and crunching on the bark of trees with their sharp incisors at night while camping on other rivers. If they stop using their teeth they grow too long, I'm told. Beavers keep their magnificent coats healthy with a "combing claw" on each hind foot and oil glands near the tail. Hunted for their beautiful pelts in the past, they were brought close to extinction.

Twenty minutes later a female emerald-green ruby-throated hummingbird swooped in. She flew backwards, straight up and down and then hovered in front of my face. I sat in speechless silence while we stared at each other—eye to eye. Her tiny wings flapped so hard and fast she sounded like a helicopter. Giving two "tweets" she zoomed away.

Since hummingbirds only weigh one-tenth of an ounce, I am in awe of how they travel five-hundred miles across the Gulf of Mexico to winter. It's no accident that the ancients considered these delicate, beautiful birds a symbol of joy and an affirmation of the magic of life. Bursting with energy they die if caged. Stirred by the hummingbird and beavers' trust, I wept. They too captured and held my heart.

"The animals don't seem afraid of me!" I cried. Doc shrugged and gave a huge smile. I reflected on each animal; something was wrung from me—a word, a gasp as I sat breathless with wonder. Although I had no photograph, they left me something better than a picture, something time could only glorify—a loving ecstasy that filled my heart when I thought of the wild.

Our hitchhiker friends, the biting flies, were less numerous also. A small brown and white wood duck darted among the reeds nearby. It looked at us unperturbed. I heard that wood ducks nest in tree cavities or in man-made nest boxes. The female lays up to fifteen eggs on a bed of white down, where she incubates the eggs for about four weeks.

The black river was getting bigger and more silent. Doc's watch thermometer showed the water was ninety degrees near the swamp, where the river was shallow and narrow and eighty degrees where it was wide and deep.

A cool breeze massaged our bodies when we stopped at a shady sandbar for lunch. Doc returned the lunch items to his canoe. His athletic-looking body was now bronzed by the sun, and his week-old beard was a forest of little silver stubble on his chin and neck. Enjoying the warm sunshine and puffs of air on our skin, we walked down the sandbar and sat in the middle of the river downstream. We were white people but felt like Indians inside.

A mockingbird called. We tried to imitate the bird, but our call sounded different. The mockingbird imitated us, making us laugh. Another grey mockingbird unfurled its white feathers as it landed on a nearby willow tree. Repeating each note exactly, it imitated the other birds.

We launched the canoes again after lunch and thought we were halfway between Fargo and Highway 6. A thin cloud cover made this the coolest day of our trip so far. The gnats buzzing around our heads sounded like mosquitoes. The drone of bees, flies, hornets and wasps became part of the background noise. Since they did not bite or sting, we ignored them.

We paddled to the west of an island where large tupelo trees stood like sentinels on a small beach. The current from a side creek thundered like a waterfall and created a sea of foam. The tupelo's tentacle-like roots were mirrored in the black water. The sun peeked out through wispy clouds to illuminate the cypress trees and their knees.

Two men and three children were fishing along the bank. A red-faced bearded man in his forties greeted us with a hand wave. "The water's high for a change," the red-faced man said with authority. "Was low last week."

"Guess we lucked out," Doc responded. "We can't touch the bottom of the river with our paddles."

"I'm going to make a pit stop," Doc yelled once we had passed.

I stopped to admire a huge live oak tree. "Thank you, green growing one, for your precious shade and beauty," I whispered patting the tree. Doc's dragon canoe floated up.

The sun was slipping towards the horizon, but we had not seen a sandbar for a couple of hours. "Oh dear, I hope we find something," I said, concerned.

A small sandbar came into view. It was no beauty but it would do. The sand spit faced a wall of soil, with fan-shaped palmettoes and tall slash pine trees along the ridge. There was a "tap, tap, tap" of a pileated woodpecker in the distance.

Making a rhythmic pounding sound on a hollow tree, the woodpecker looks for insects to stab with the spear-like point of its long slender tongue. I was fascinated to learn that woodpeckers mate for life and share the duty of raising young during their twelve-year life-span.

We pitched the tent. Our four-and-a-half hour paddle had left us exhausted. Doc snored softly on the tarp while he napped. Refreshed after floating on my back in the river, I went exploring.

Rustling sounds came from a nearby palmetto grove. The tiny footprints and tail drags of the nine-banded armadillo covered the sand. Following the tracks and noise I peered under a bush and froze. An armadillo was sniffing under leaves with its small head and long squarish snout. While admiring its lizard-like skin and bony-plated shell that protects it from predators, I moved slightly and betrayed myself. It sniffed the air and paused before it skittered off for cover.

I heard that the female armadillo gives birth each year to quadruplets which are always the same sex, and that they are extending their range northwards.

Sitting at the water's edge, I drew strength from the river's peace. Although there were a lot of clouds, there was no sign of a storm.

"Niki, come and look at this!" Doc pointed to the slender brown body of a large dragon fly with four transparent wings. It was holding an empty husk. The abdomen must have lengthened as two pairs of crumpled wings unfolded when it emerged from its nymph case. To catch mosquitoes they make a basket-like trap with their legs in flight.

The next morning we paddled single file between steep twenty-foot banks covered with carpets of soft moss. Springs emptied into the river with a pleasant trickling sound. Dizzy with joy, I inhaled a cool breath of mist.

"Ka-ploosh," a beaver slapped its tail on the water's surface. I jumped in surprise. The beaver's tiny fury head made a V-shape in the water when it swam among the ripples down river.

Two men, the same fishermen we had seen the previous day, were putting canoes in the river at a boat landing. "Where's your side kick?" asked the red-haired man. "Didn't I see you with another person yesterday?"

"Oh, he's up river," I yelled. "Is this a public boat ramp?"

"Yeah, it's Rowland's Landing. It's five miles north of Highway 6," said the other man.

A boy and girl came running up. "Tell her about the alligator, Daddy!" the wide-eyed girl insisted.

"Yeah, we saw an eight foot alligator a few minutes ago," the red-haired man said gravely. I laughed.

We stopped for lunch on a sandbar shaded by a grove of "ogeechee goomie gums," Doc's nick-name for tupelo trees. The men paddled past us clattering and chattering, towing rubber rafts and coolers. They were in separate canoes, each with a woman and child. "We might get there next year," the red-haired man yelled with a smile.

"Come on, Daddy ... faster," shouted the boy sitting in the center of his canoe; his father grinned back. The women sat stone-faced in the front of the canoes while the men paddled.

Back on the river, Doc and I paddled together hugging the shore line for shade. A huge white sandbar with high bluffs and a grove of old cypress trees came into view. Captivated by the mountain of sparkling sand, we decided to spend the night.

A biblical-looking setting sun sent shafts of light streaming down from gold trimmed clouds. We washed our hair and then floated motionless on our backs in the shallows. The cold water made our bodies tingle with aliveness in the warm breeze. To our delight, the place was riddled with fresh game tracks. We followed a couple of raccoon and deer tracks through the brush.

"Bang, bang, bang," came the sound of someone firing a gun repeatedly. "I think they are doing target practice," Doc said, noticing my concerned look. There was the soft muffled sound of a car engine on the opposite bank. A jeep jerked and shuddered as it slowly wound its way along a bumpy dirt road.

A nearby owl call was answered by another from farther away. Their haunting duet echoed on the wind. Soft rumblings and flickering lightning came from the eastern horizon when thunder clouds gathered. A gentle drizzle turned into a hard rain. Watching the flitting wall of water from under the umbrella, I became lost in a reverie. When I closed my eyes, I felt as if I were floating, held aloft by a cloud. In the wild I have flashes of self-forgetfulness—holy moments that seem to purify my soul.

If I have to worship God, it's going to be in the temple that His hands made....Climb the mountains and get their good tidings. Nature's peace will flow into you as sunshine flows into trees. The winds will blow their freshness into you, and the storms their energy, while cares drop off like autumn leaves.

John Muir

CHAPTER 6

BIG SHOALS

The day of my spiritual awakening was the day I saw, and knew I saw all things in God and God in all things.

Mechtild of Magdeburg

When I urinated before going to bed, I felt a burning, itching pain.

"I think I have a yeast infection," I confided in Doc.

"Oh no," Doc said concerned. "Perhaps it'll be gone in the morning."

"I wish," I said wistfully and fell asleep. I left the tent to tinkle during the night. It still hurt.

"Scat! ... scat!" Doc yelled when I got in the tent.

"It's only me," I whispered with a giggle.

"I thought you were a raccoon," Doc chuckled.

The next morning the pain was worse. "I definitely have an infection."

"What should we do?" Doc asked nervously.

"Well, we can hitch a ride back to your van from the Highway 6 bridge or we can paddle twenty five miles to White Springs. I vote for White Springs."

Doc glanced at me furtively. "That's fine with me," he said packing his sleeping bag.

A small spotted brown fawn exploded from the water and ran up the steep sandbank as my canoe drew near. I smiled with pure pleasure. When we stopped for lunch an owl flew over us and crossed the river. We gaped after it.

I wore sandals, but after going barefoot so much, wearing my sandals made me feel I'd lost one of my senses. The texture of the sand, leaves, roots and stones had felt good on the soles of my feet. Now all I felt was rubber.

Moving about two miles an hour, we estimated we had paddled six miles. We expected to paddle twelve miles that day and thirteen the next and anticipated going straight to the emergency room when we got to White Springs the following evening.

Back on the river Doc took pictures of a high terraced bluff with two springs cascading down fern-strewn rocks to form a waterfall. Two brown-and-white striped baby alligators about a foot in length lay on a grassy shore. My pulse beat faster. We knew their mother was watching somewhere.

We pitched the tent on a sandy island. After paddling sixteen miles in six hours, I was exhausted. Feeling sick and vulnerable, I began to tear up. Doc gave me a hug. "Doc, don't look so worried," I chided. It felt good to weep like last night's rain. We thought of ways to get to the emergency room once we got to White Springs.

An old dark blue pickup truck came to a halt on the opposite bank. A woman who looked in her forties and a man who seemed to be in his early twenties hopped out. They unloaded their camping gear on a small beach and began to put up a large tent. Thirty minutes later they were still working on the tent.

"Would you like some help?" Doc offered.

"No thanks," the woman yelled, "We're going to put the tent up or kill each other." The young man was thin and silent; she was overweight and friendly. I liked her. She wore a red top and white shorts, he a camouflage shirt and pants. They finally got their tent up and started to play country music.

"It could be worse; they could be playing rock," I confided. There was a pleasant tinkle of cascading water from a small shoal upstream. When an older man joined our neighbors, we thought he might be the woman's husband while the young man was their son. "How did you know about the beach?" I yelled across the river.

"The land is leased by a hunting club," the woman shouted back. Our island was so small we had to be creative finding privacy to go to the bathroom.

It was a rough night. The pain and fear made me shiver. Feeling desperate and thinking it more than a coincidence that we had neighbors when I needed aid, I resolved to ask for help. At first light I changed clothes and went to tinkle. The pick up truck's diesel engine started up. I paddled over in a hurry. The older man looked grave when he met me.

"Excuse me. Are you going into town?" I asked blinking back tears. "I need medical attention." The woman joined us.

The man turned to the woman, "Go stop David; he can take her to the emergency room." She dashed off and returned a few moment later.

"You're in luck," she said. "My son was just heading off to work." I gave a sigh of relief.

David's pick up truck gave a "chug, chug" sound while he drove. He was quiet and answered my questions with a "yes ma'am, no ma'am."

"I'll get someone to pick you up around eight," he said when he dropped me off at the Lake City Hospital emergency room. It was seven.

Except for a man with a bandaged hand, the waiting room was empty. It felt strange to be back in civilization, and I worried about getting a ride back. The kindness of these people was touching.

My doctor was a tall, tanned, slender young woman with blue eyes and an English accent. She said she was from New Zealand but lived in Jacksonville, Florida. "I've been in the States twelve years now, but I was actually born in Chicago. The economy has gone to pot in New Zealand. It used to be nice," she said wistfully. "Where are you from?" she asked from behind the sheet draped across my knees. Lying on my back I could not see her.

"I grew up in South Africa, but I've been in the States eighteen years," I muttered in the direction of the sheet.

"Oh, you're in the same situation. I thought I heard an English accent."

"Yeah, I was born in New Orleans."

"Wow, we have a lot in common," she bubbled peering into the microscope. "You have a yeast infection," she said softly. "I'll give you suppositories."

At eight-thirty I was still waiting outside the emergency room. Knowing what was wrong made me feel better. The traffic had picked up, but there was no sign of a ride. I listened for every truck that went "chug, chug" like David's, but none appeared. My prescription also needed to be filled, but the Prescription Place, a pharmacy down the road, didn't open until nine. It occurred to me to leave a message that I was at the pharmacy, but I decided to wait.

A young woman wearing sun glasses stopped in a muddy white pick-up truck at nine. "Are you Niki?" she stammered. "I'm Melissa. I'm a neighbor of David and his parents, and I can take you back to camp." Blinking back grateful tears, I got into the truck.

"I need to get a prescription filled," I confided.

"No problem. We'll try Kmart. It's cheaper and just down the road." The store was closed. We tried Wal-Mart and Eckerd Drugs. All were closed. Returning to the emergency room, we stopped at the Prescription Place, but the door was locked. The light was on so I peered into the store. A heavy-set man at the till looked up, walked over and unlocked the door. "The store is closed," he said firmly. "July fourth is a holiday."

"Oh no!" I said despondently.

"Okay, I'll fill your prescription!" He sighed scratching his gray hair.

"Whew," I gasped.

"I appreciate your doing this," I told Melissa.

"Glad to," Melissa declared. "I've been through a lot too. I just got divorced and lost all that I owned," she murmured. She was twenty-four and had no children.

The overweight woman greeted us when we got to the river. She introduced herself as Bonnie and her husband as John. "What did the doctor say?" she asked protectively.

"I have a yeast infection," I mumbled, embarrassed. Doc and John walked up. Bonnie hesitated. She looked as if she'd like to pursue the subject further but changed her mind.

"Where did you put your canoes in?" Bonnie asked looking at Doc.

"Just south of the Okefenokee swamp," Doc blurted.

Bonnie looked at her husband, "That's John's dream," she bubbled. "But I couldn't spend that much time with him." We all laughed. We waved good-bye to Melissa, Bonnie and John about thirty minutes later.

The river was wide with steep banks. Two large alligators sank amid silver bubbles before I got close. Black storm clouds moved in, and the wind began to howl. Doc caught up with me just as a pounding rain blotted out the world. Paddling under a tunnel of trees, we cut down on the angry gusts and rain. Lightning and thunder claps split the heavens vertically. My pulse quickened.

The clouds had dissolved into a haze when we arrived at Big Shoals Wild Life Management Area. A sign hung across the river, "Danger: one mile to Big Shoals." We planned to portage our canoes and gear, as the canoe guide book said it was a class IV rapid and should only be run by experts. The large trees, grassy field and trail looked interesting so we got out to stretch. A huge watermelon sat on the bank. Doc examined it. "The lower part has hardened. It's been here awhile. I think we should take it."

"Hope we're not stealing," I said, a little unsure.

A half mile downstream, another warning sign hung across the river: "Dangerous rapid, only for experts." I tightened my grip on the paddle. "You can see we're approaching the falls," Doc laughed nervously. "The river is slow and sluggish. I bet it's a twenty-foot drop." When we rounded the river bend a continuous thunder announced the fall's presence.

"As the Indians say, 'It's a good day to die'," I chuckled. Doc grinned. A trail paralleled the river on the left. We pulled the canoes on land and walked down a well-worn path to the rapid. Sounding like a fleet of jumbo jets taking off, large volumes of water poured down a narrow chute to the right. Boiling and roaring, the river rushed over a series of drops.

"We can negotiate some of the smaller rapids to the left if we drag the canoes over the rocks," Doc said pointing to a chain of smaller rapids.

Four hours of paddling had left me exhausted and in pain. "Can we deal with the rapid tomorrow?" I pleaded.

"I'm really anxious to get it over with," Doc countered. "The longer I wait, the more nervous I get."

"Okay," I moaned and collapsed in the river to cool off. We walked back to our canoes and tied down the gear. "I'm really keyed up now," Doc said anxiously.

Paddling slowly, Doc went down the first rapid. I followed. His boat jammed against the rocks and stopped. Going around him, I slid down another chute. "Crunch," came the sound of my canoe hitting the rocks.

"Push your canoe to the left," Doc yelled.

"Mind your own boat!" I exclaimed. A feeling of calm came over me. I got out and pushed the canoe. Getting in, I slid into the next trough. I repeated the procedure until my canoe became tightly wedged between two rocks. Remaining seated, I watched Doc's boat slip gracefully down the next couple of rapids.

Two women on the shore stopped to observe us, their beached canoes visible up river. "Would you like a shove?" the shorter woman offered, looking at me. She hopped across the rocks and pushed. With a thrill of excitement I shot forward and slid down a huge drop into a pool. Water sloshed into my canoe with a loud splash.

A sea of foam floated rapidly in the current at a large white sandbar below the falls. The roar from the rapids sounded like a distant ocean. Stretching my aching legs, I stepped bare-footed on the soft sand and pitched the tent on top of the bank.

From my high vantage point I noticed some reeds moving on the opposite shore. Suddenly the reeds parted and without a sound, an otter climbed out of the water and streaked up a creek. Its furry sleek brown body glinted in the sunlight. Feeling a rush of pure energy, I sat down.

Delightful memories came to mind of other otters chirping and whistling as they played tag, rolled in the reeds and slid down muddy banks. Fast swimmers with streamlined bodies and webbed toes, they feed on fish, frogs and crayfish.

Looking around for Doc, I spied him talking with three fishermen downstream. Our sandbar had no animal tracks, only human footprints, I noticed with regret. We had dinner with watermelon for dessert, then bathed in the foamy pools among the rocks. Doc shaved while I brushed my teeth in the semi-darkness.

With my health back I felt great. "It doesn't get any better than this," I sighed. The river smelt of weeds and sulfur, and the rapids murmured softly in the background. A mosquito landed on my hand. "Mosquitoes are out," I groaned. In the tent we fell asleep listening to the big-voiced chorus of crickets, frogs and cicadas.

We woke with the chirping of birds. The pink blur of sunrise was visible through the black tree silhouettes. White froth floated across the inky river when we left camp at daybreak. We paddled up Robinson Creek, a nearby stream, under cool shady trees and stopped to gape at a waterfall that dropped thirty-feet into a small pool.

In two hours we counted five dark scaly alligators gliding across the Suwannee's black water. They sank long before we got near them, descending slowly like tiny submarines—first their body, then the snout, finally their eyes. Sometimes only one wary eye was visible. "We're seeing one alligator over and over," Doc said laughing.

"You wish!" I giggled. Paddling ahead, I slipped under a tree limb and looked up. A small reddish brown owl with ear tufts sat on a branch two feet from my head. With eyes in front like a person, it gazed at me. Then our eyes locked. Turning its head all the way around, it seemed to look through and into me. There was a huge rush in my chest. Exploding in ecstasy, I began to sob. The moment was supreme; the owl at that second seemed the most beautiful being on earth.

Doc paddled over, but the owl with its soft down wispy feathers had silently flown. "It was an owl," I stammered. "We really *saw* each other!"

"What kind of owl?

"It was little, with soft black eyes, ear tufts and spots," I whispered still hallowed by its presence.

"It sounds like a screech owl," Doc said thoughtfully. The tears kept flowing, joyful tears that made me feel soft and open.

The first time I heard the quavering, eerie wail of the screech owl my hair stood on end. Because an owl can see in the dark, it was called the night eagle by our ancestors and was associated with death, clairvoyance or wisdom. The companion owl of Athena, the Greek Goddess of wisdom, could reveal unseen truths.

A small white egret with a yellow bill walked along the bank. Instead of flying off, it faced us with its beak open.

Between 1875 and 1914 when the plumes used by the male to woo its mate were in fashion for women's hats, egrets were almost exterminated by hunters. Although they can live up to fourteen years and have come back from the brink, they are still threatened by drought, drainage and real estate development.

When we stopped for breakfast on a white shady sandbar the river was wide, deep and sluggish with steep banks. There were more human footprints and garbage. Attractive houses were nestled in among the trees about two miles north of White Springs, and huge rocks, ferns, and tall trees covered the bluffs.

We stopped at River Road, a canoe rental outfit at White Springs. Nobody was home. Their rental flyer had a quotation by Stephen Williams, the owner: "The Suwannee carries a message back to each of us in the echo of her name. I believe there is special meaning in this river. In her turns and shadows we who would perceive the course of nature and its balance will better know ourselves."

After lunch we left our canoes under White Springs's state road 136 bridge and walked four blocks to a grocery. White Springs was an attractive, quiet town with well-manicured lawns and live oak trees covered in Spanish moss. The people greeted us with a friendly "hello." I bought fresh fruit and vegetables while Doc made some phone calls.

"I talked to my ex-wife," Doc said clearing his throat. "My boxer is fine." He gave me a sidelong glance. "I also talked to Amy," he said in a distant voice. "She found out I was canoeing with you and broke up with me." He gave a sheepish grin.

We walked back to the canoes. "How do you feel about losing Amy?" I asked looking at him.

"Okay. I guess I had it coming!" He swallowed and forced a smile.

Two men and a woman were sitting in yellow sea kayaks near our canoes. "Where did you put in?" I asked the group.

"At Fargo. We've been on the river three days," a sandy-haired man in his thirties said, getting out of his kayak.

"How many miles are you doing?" I asked with interest.

"About two hundred and fifty. We're doing seventeen miles a day—it's a lot. I'd do it differently next time," he confessed. They were from Marianna, Florida. The men worked at a boys' school for juvenile delinquents, and the woman was a nurse. They said they had dinner with a family camped across from a sandy island the previous night. We decided they had dinner with Bonnie and John, the couple who had helped me to get medical attention. When the kayakers went to the grocery store, we paddled another hour and then stopped to swim at a small sandbar flanked by twenty-foot limestone bluffs.

Curious about the tunnels of mounded sand that snaked in and out of the water along the shore, we burrowed into the earth but found nothing. A man's footprints were on the sandbar, I noted with curiosity. He had stopped to urinate, for the sand was wet in front of his last set of footprints.

My red life jacket was gone. Troubled by its loss, I searched everywhere, then forgot about it. After the three kayakers had passed, we pitched the tent under a live oak tree. When the sun's fiery ball slid below the horizon the air became cool. The river mirrored the trees, the bluffs, our canoes and us.

The hum of a motor boat approaching from up river broke the silence. A man appeared. "Where is Blue Sink Springs?" he hollered slowing down.

"Not sure," Doc answered.

"Where ya'll from?" the man yelled.

"Atlanta," Doc replied.

"I go there all the time. I'm in the parts business," he shouted before disappearing around the river bend. Deep shadows crept across the canyon, and yellow and pink clouds reflected in the river's jet black surface.

The crickets and cicadas began their chorus. There was a pattern to their plaintiff songs. A slow start with a few creaking and grinding voices, then the whole orchestra rising to a crescendo. An eerie silence. Then the chorus began again: the song of the smoky-winged cicadas on the right, the piping crickets, rubbing their forewings against their hind wings, on the left; the deep sonorous mating calls of male frogs; and a side melody from the elusive mottled brown whip-poor-will. Calling its name, another whip-poor-will echoed the first, upstream. The frogs rivaled the bird song in volume but not in sweetness.

"Plop-splash," a silver bass struck the water's surface. A bushy-tailed gray squirrel rustled the leaves of the trees while it jumped from limb to limb. Muffled rumbling sounds also came from the cars traveling on the interstate two-and-a-half miles away.

Listening in breathless awe, I stopped thinking. It was as if I had lost my mind and come to my senses. Above the deep orange western horizon was the tiny wisp of a new moon frozen in the sky. The fading light lit up the wakes of the water bugs as they darted across the inky water. Their trails twinkled like a million stars.

When we started down river the next morning, something red hung on a submerged log. Relieved, I realized it was my life jacket. We paddled one-and-a-half miles farther and stopped for breakfast.

"Hey, Niki, look here," Doc yelled pointing to a tiny insect under his leg at the water's edge. "It makes the sand tunnels near the water." We examined the bug more closely. It had a hairy long brown two-part body with short wings, a head with a short antenna, lobster-like claws, and grasshopper-like legs. We later learned it's called a mole cricket.

"Mystery solved," I said with astonishment.

When we got back on the river a brownish-yellow female cardinal with a prominent crest followed my canoe along the bank. Her bright red mate with black around his eyes and bill was nowhere in sight.

A large brown osprey flew by with a fish in its claws. We stared spellbound. The hum of interstate cars to the north became louder. On our right, Swift Creek's water rushed between tall limestone bluffs and emptied into the Suwannee. When we approached the I-75 bridge the automobiles thundered past. Swallows that made a home underneath the bridge dove and twittered around us. We looked around. The river now meandered between towering white limestone cliffs.

Ducks exploded from the water in front of a tall snow-white sandbar. A flat shady area on top of the sandy hill became our home for the night. The gleaming black river snaked through white limestone canyons below our camp. Live oak, maple, sweet gum, elm, white birch and willow trees dotted the shore. Spanish moss hung among the tree branches, fluttering gracefully in the breeze. Green resurrection fern hugged many of the tree limbs. The plant is named "resurrection fern" as it turns from brown to green after a rain.

Behind the sandbar we located the one-thousand, three-hundred mile long foot trail developed by the Florida Trail Association. Fifty miles of it follows the Suwannee.

After dinner we set up our tent and then porpoised through the water to cool off. A storm threatened at dusk, but the clouds stopped just south of us. Our camp seemed magical. Paradise had not been lost; it had been found!

On our last day, we planned to leave the river at Live Oak and estimated we had a two-hour paddle. After three hours of paddling our boats, Live Oak was still nowhere in sight. The long broad wings of a soaring eagle came into view while we were having lunch. Gazing up at its magnificent flight, it seemed to be God-in-Hiding. Stirred by the eagle, I reflected on how our ancestors believed the eagle was sacred because it connected us with the divine. Eagle medicine, according to many Native Americans, is realized when we turn life's trials into personal power and live in balance with the Spirit and Earth realms. The eagle's presence seemed like a good omen and a sign that my spirit was fulfilling itself.

When I arrived at Live Oak ahead of Doc an hour later, people were lazing on a long white sandy beach. A dark-haired woman in a red bathing suit raised her fist in the air and shouted, "Up with woman power!"

"Yeah!" I yelled, raising my fist in the air.

She turned to Doc and hissed, "She's stronger than you!" Doc narrowed his eyes and looked amused. What a lovely moment: it felt good to be an inspiration to my sisters, just as other women had inspired me. Yes, indeed, up with woman power!

We rounded a bend and my eyes fell on the remains of the stone wall of Suwannee Springs, a popular health spa where people came to swim and drink the mineral water at the turn of the century.

Stephen Foster State Park, located on the north bank, has a two-hundred foot Carillon Tower which houses one of the world's largest sets of tubular bells. Foster's music is played every hour on the hour.

I beached my canoe. "Where can I find a phone?" I asked a young man with sunglasses.

"Down the dirt road at the store. I'll give you a ride," he said pulling out his car keys. Doc ambled up and asked him about Suwannee Springs. "There's a better spring downriver with Indian artifacts," he said amiably.

We were drifting in the current on our backs when the man with whom we had left the truck arrived. It was sad to say good-bye to the wilderness and load the canoes on the van. Wanting more nature, I did not look forward to going back to work.

When I drove to the clinic the next morning the dead body of a deer lay by the side of the road. My rear view mirror told the grisly tale. A streak of blood led from the deer to a point in the road. "I am so sorry, deer," I cried. I did not like civilization much.

The following weekend I met a hunter at a picnic. He used powder guns, archery and shot-guns to hunt deer, duck, and rabbit. "I have a problem with hunting," I said apologetically. Then deluge ... "hunting is necessary, the animals have no predators ... we need to keep the numbers in check ..." He went on and on about all the virtues of hunting. My mind went blank, I wanted to run, I wanted to cry. Was I going crazy?

At home I realized there was no such thing as a "wild" animal. I loved all animals like a trusting puppy. I could not kill a pet, and all wild animals had become my companions. No, more than that, they were God-in-Hiding. We all were.

I dreamed of the Suwannee every night for two weeks. The magic of the river filled my soul, infiltrated my cells. I longed to be back in the wild, where life was simple, where the pulse of Great Spirit could be felt everywhere.

Doc and I started making plans to canoe the Everglades in December. The idea of doing the hundred-mile Wilderness Waterway excited me.

CHAPTER 7

THE EVERGLADES

And if you would know God, be not therefore a solver of riddles.
Rather look about you and you shall see Him playing with your children.
And look into space; you shall see Him walking in the cloud,
outstretching His arms in the lightning and descending in rain.
You shall see Him smiling in flowers, then rising and waving His hands
in trees.

Kahlil Gibran

For me Christmas is best spent in the Great Outdoors beyond the world of calendars. It is a gift of time to find the timeless in a place where I feel the seamless kinship with all things.

After a year of anticipation, research and planning, Christmas in the Everglades of Florida was finalized. My partner, Doc, and I were to paddle the hundred-mile Wilderness Waterway. Then my worst nightmare. A week before we were due to leave, Doc got sick and had to cancel. "Call Jay Heath; he'd like to go," Doc said, trying to ease my disappointment."

Canoeing with someone I'd not met was a concern, but my fears subsided when I talked to Jay on the phone. We discussed the challenges—the endurance required to paddle a hundred miles across vast, breezy bays and against tidal rivers; turning over in the boat; being vulnerable to hypothermia; having to drag the canoe across sharp oyster beds in waist-deep mud; getting lost. The guidebooks also caution against salt-water mosquitos, alligators, crocodiles, sharks, and raccoons that steal food and bite holes in water containers for fresh water. Although the park service recommends that inexperienced boaters use a guide, we thought we would learn to navigate on our own. We agreed to use my car, canoe and charts.

70 Earth, the Forgotten Temple

A cold front with below-freezing temperatures approached the Southeast two days before our departure. When I expressed fear at work that my house's water pipes might freeze, my colleagues recommended I turn my water off before leaving. My phone was ringing when I got home that evening. "So you're going to turn your water off," my friend, John, said solemnly.

"How did you know?" I asked in surprise. "We haven't talked in over a month."

"I just thought you might," he said amiably. Then in a more serious tone. "Be sure to turn off your hot water heater. The element could burn out."

"You're an angel; I didn't know." His advice seemed like a sign of divine intervention. Other things fell into place. We found an outfitter to do the hundred fifty-mile shuttle, and the local ranger said we would not have trouble getting camping permits over Christmas.

Jay arrived at my house after lunch on December 22, 1989 to leave for the trip. His brown eyes and furrowed brow were hidden behind thick-rimmed glasses. While I drove, we talked about ourselves in an effort to get to know each other. Even with our common interest in outdoor adventures, the conversation began to lag. A couple of hours later we were silent.

After a seven-hour drive, we spent the first night at an Econo Lodge just south of Tampa, Florida. When we arrived at Everglades City the following morning, a park ranger persuaded us not to leave that day, for gale-force winds and below freezing temperatures were expected. We reserved campsites for nine nights starting the next day, December 24, and slept at the Captain's Table Hotel.

According to the weather report that evening, the I-75 and I-95 interstates were closed because of heavy snow in north Florida. Our having reached Everglades City before the bad weather seemed like a sign that the trip was meant to be. However, my apprehension increased when I looked over our two large waterproof charts of the Everglades. A hundred miles seemed a long way, paddling two miles an hour, about ten miles a day, for ten days.

My anxiety intensified at the Chokoloskee launch site at daybreak. A local fisherman told Jay how to exit the bay, while I went to an outfitter who charged us a hundred-and-fifty dollars to drive my car to the Flamingo Ranger station where the trip would end.

The sun, pale and watery, peeked out from behind gray misty clouds, when we headed for Lopez River, our first campsite, with a heavy load of gear plus fifteen gallons of water. Sitting only a couple of inches above the water line, the canoe threatened to overturn each time we moved. My heart fluttered in my chest.

The icy, howling twenty-five-knot northwest tailwind pushed us across the white foamy waves. My rain jacket flapped in the gusts sounding like a paddle boat. My breath quickened. Our sixteen-foot green Mohawk canoe was a tiny speck in the vast gray bay.

The boat veered to the right. I swallowed and looked around. "Jay, steer to the left," I stammered, for he controlled the canoe's direction from the stern.

"I am!" he yelled, his face hardening. He narrowed his eyes and stared at the horizon. "At least we won't drown," he hissed.

Chuckling, I began to relax. He was right; the bay was only a few feet deep. "Crunch," came the sickening sound of the canoe grounding itself on an oyster bar. I cast about wildly. We talked of pulling the canoe to deeper water, but the razor edged shells could cut our feet when the sticky, low oxygenated mud gripped our shoes. We studied the water for another route. Paddling backwards, we found a deeper channel. Relieved, we allowed the shrieking wind to drive us forward without effort for five miles.

Located on the southwest tip of Florida, the up to seventy-eight-mile-wide Everglades National Park starts at Lake

Okeechobee and ends a hundred miles south at the Gulf. Nearly half of the Everglades lies in three-foot tidal flats with scattered islands or "hammocks" of trees and shrubs dotting the mostly sawgrass and mangrove wilderness. The slow, shallow, fifty-mile-wide, freshwater Everglades River flows southwest towards the Gulf, covering only one-and-a-half miles per day.

The northwestern section of the Everglades is named the "Ten Thousand Island" region because the river meanders through a labyrinth of mangrove keys. The sturdy aerial roots of evergreen red mangrove trees, freshwater plants that have gone to sea, bind the nutrient-rich silt to build new land and act as a nursery for mollusks, crustaceans, fish and algae. The brackish hundred-mile Wilderness Waterway alternates between narrow rivers and wide, shimmering bays.

For the last thirty million years the sea has ebbed and flowed over the Florida Plateau, changing its shape. Florida's shoreline extended farther seaward when the ocean levels dropped around three hundred feet during the ice ages some ten to twelve thousand years ago. The warm climate and absence of glaciers probably account for the mastodons, mammoths, giant ground sloths, saber-toothed tigers and llamas that once roamed Florida during the ice ages. The fossils of many extinct mammals, birds, reptiles and amphibians are still being found in Florida today.

Two hours later, we set up our tents at Lopez River, our island campsite. I felt a surge of elation. Lopez River's broad, brown, shallow water sparkled in sunlight. To warm up we lazed on a crushed gray and white oyster shell beach along the bank. The oyster shell's dark-ridged tops, their white insides and the purple scar where the edible mollusk was once attached gave the beach a colorful look.

Our camp was a small flat land clearing with two picnic tables, a chemical toilet, and clusters of sword-like green-leafed mother-in-law tongue plants. Tall black mangroves with thick green elliptical leaves and pencil-thin knees grew in the high tide zone.

Two ghost crabs with jointed legs, squarish shells and long stalk-like eyes with three hundred and sixty-degree vision sprinted across the mud on their toes. The bigger crab, a male, waved its large pincer that serves as a weapon and a mating signal. I heard that crabs breathe by passing oxygen-laden water through their gill chambers. When a gray, white and black Ring-Billed Gull with yellow legs swooped towards us, the crab disappeared into a hole.

A television program from the previous night had helped ease my apprehension about the trip. When things got desperate, a Borneo adventurer, who had walked through mud and befriended headhunters, taped a message to his daughter about not being crazy but a prisoner of his dreams. I, too, felt like a prisoner of my dreams; I needed adventure; I needed to take risks, to expand, and to learn.

A small long-beaked marsh wren with a whitish breast and dark brown wings sat on a mangrove branch a few feet from my head. Hopping nimbly among the leaves, it picked with its long curved beak at a seed that looked like a black-eyed pea. The rustle of leaves, the wind's roar on the bay water, and the call of gulls could not fill the great silence.

With the strong winds and freezing temperatures we doubted whether the three other canoeists scheduled to share the campsite that night would show. However, when the last of the sun's rays shifted through the mangrove branches like falling leaves, two men and a boy arrived in a couple of canoes. The solo canoeist staggered towards us. "We canoed thirteen miles into the wind. We're soaked and exhausted," he groaned.

"Our boat turned over near Watson's Place and we got lost and paddled in a circle between markers 126 and 127," lamented the boy, who was the solo paddler's son. They were from Virginia and planned to go to Everglades City the next day, then drive to Flamingo by car to canoe around there.

74 Earth, the Forgotten Temple

When I went to bed I had a knot in my stomach, and I thought seriously about turning back.

Golden rays of sunshine and puffs of wind hallowed us on Christmas day, lifting my spirits. "Crunch!" The canoe ran aground at the first channel intersection. I jumped reflexively, and yanked the charts out. Jay and I debated about routes. We went around the shallow area, and the next marker came into view. We sighed with relief.

Our rain-jackets rattled, and the water hissed in the freshening breeze. Aided by the blustering twenty-knot northwesterly tailwind, our boat seem to fly across the flat, gleaming waters of Sunday, Oyster and Last Huston Bays for ten miles. But the wind hurled its full fury on our boat's nose when we left the Wilderness Waterway and turned northeast the last two miles. It snatched at our heaving paddles until our arms ached.

We were relieved when we found Sweetwater Bay's two elevated ten by twelve-foot wooden platforms built for camping. The roofed platforms, also known as chickees, were separated by a chemical toilet housed in a small wooden building and stood in the water away from the mangroves behind a circular island.

We tied the canoe behind the platform and listened to the "lap ... lap" sound of water in the wind and an occasional "thud" as the canoe hit the chickee. Tree leaves rustled and nesting birds chattered nearby. A dark gray six-foot alligator floated in front of us, then gently sank like a submarine.

The alligators in the Everglades are growing only one-third the weight of their relatives. Their maximum weight is two hundred pounds instead of six hundred, and they take four times as long, up to twenty years, to reach reproduction maturity. In studying their stomach contents a researcher found they live mostly on water snakes and salamanders and not fish, raccoons and other animals. The declining wildlife is blamed on the Everglades becoming more tidal when the natural flow of fresh water was interrupted, and on high levels of mercury pollution coming from faraway smokestacks that falls in rain.

Jay groaned and sighed when he put up his tent. He said he was forty but his stooped shoulders and his shuffled gait made him seem older. Three large scaly alligators glided across the bay with only their heads visible. All was well; the wind had been behind us; my canoe partner was a good paddler, and I had the solitude I needed.

Two weary-looking blonde-haired German women arrived as the amber sun slid below the horizon. They took the second chickee. "We canoed over sixteen miles today from Chokoloskee and lost our way," the taller woman confided in a German accent. Relieved to be in before dark, they danced in a circle and sang in German. They were exchange students and had been in the States three months.

The wind died at dusk, and everything became still in the darkness. Looking up at the stars, I felt a strange power—of being part of something much bigger than myself.

"Let's see what a good outdoors woman you are. Where's the north star?" Jay asked looking towards the northern horizon.

"I don't know. The stars are great lights of mystery," I said smiling.

"I never can find it!" he muttered peering towards the north.

The German women were still in their tent when we left the Sweetwater Bay Chickee at first light. Three grayish-colored five-foot-long bottle-nosed dolphins with prominent dorsal fins leapt and dove next to our canoe for a quarter mile in Chevelier Bay. They darted under the bow and rocked the boat when they swam around us. With a deep sighing sound they surfaced to exhale explosively through a small blow-hole near the top of their heads, then rapidly inhaled before diving again. They must break water periodically to breathe or they will drown. The dolphins seemed to be smiling with their open beak-like toothy jaws.

Using sonar to navigate and find food, dolphins emit a steady stream of high-pitched clicks, which bounce off objects and echo back, giving them a sophisticated "sound-picture" of their surroundings. Research shows that humans have a greater production in T-cells and endorphins which boost the immune system, and a slower heartbeat when around dolphins. People who swim with dolphins also report experiencing their echolocation energy moving up their spines, resulting in a feeling of deep relaxation and joy. Dolphins are warm blooded, bear live young which they nurse and are affectionate, often stroking each others' soft, smooth, sensitive skin with their flippers.

"Hello ... I love you!" I called, and thought how for centuries sailors have considered their presence a good omen and how the ancient Greeks honored them as gods. The word "dolphin" has its roots in the Greek word "delphi" meaning womb.

The larger dolphin lifted its short projecting snout to look at us. I'm told dolphins can see in air and water because their eye muscles and lenses enable them to see light rays and focus. One of the dolphins flipped a fish in the air with its snout. Speeding away from us, the other caught the fish, and flicked it back. With tails moving in an undulating motion, not sideways like most fish, they dove and leapt cutting across the water. Being fast swimmers, these small relatives of the whale can swim up to thirty miles per hour.

The day broke clear, but a cold wind from the north soon blew in clouds and it began to drizzle. I put on a poncho and placed a tarp across the gear. "My rain gear is buried; I'll just have to get wet," Jay moaned. Because of the freezing temperatures, many of the fish were dying; some were already dead and had washed up on the banks while others wallowed on the surface, their bodies turning somersaults. I felt a dull, empty ache while I watched.

An osprey sat on a huge stick nest piled a foot high in a tree in Alligator Bay. Through the binoculars I could see its large brown neck and head. Another osprey hovered ahead of us and then plunged, feet first, into the water locking its talons into a large silver fish. Once endangered, osprey have begun to recover from the effects of pesticides and pollutants.

Alligator and Plate creeks were narrow and looked like lush tropical forests with palmettos, mangroves and air-plants. Tiny rainbows glistened in the beads of dew that clung to the leaves of the green leafy pineapple-like airplants nestled among the mangrove branches. The airplants absorb nutrients from the water collected in their cup-shaped base. The mangroves' arched wet air-breathing roots formed little jungles of sparkling pipes. Water swilling through the mangroves' knee-like roots and spikes shimmered on the underside of their thick waxy leaves.

After an easy ten-and-a-half-mile paddle, we arrived at the Plate Creek Chickee. Golden shafts of sunlight broke through the gray clouds. The tide turned while we were sitting on the dock at Plate Creek. A loud squealing sound came from across the bay. We jumped up to look. Four tiny yellowish-brown piglets strutted across the far bank. I dove for my binoculars, but the piglets disappeared in a thicket.

I had heard that the pigs, one of the most intelligent of animals, are the descendents of domestic pigs brought by the European explorers.

A motor boat with two men and a boy sped towards us and stopped. "Mind if we use your toilet?" asked a man wearing an insulated army jacket.

"No, go ahead," we said nodding in the direction of the toilets.

"Feels good to stretch the ol' legs!" said the other man. They were from Lakeland, Florida and had been coming here for eighteen years to fish.

The man with the insulated army jacket joined us. "You bein out in this god-awful weather?"

"Yeah," Jay said proudly. They expressed sadness about the snook, a popular gamefish, dying from the cold. The long silver snook with its protruding lower jaw and two separate dorsal fins puts up a ferocious fight when caught.

"Is it okay to eat the dead fish?" I asked.

"Only if their gills are red," said the man in the army jacket. "Wouldn't advise eating the oysters," he added.

"Did ya know each other b'fore this trip?" the other man asked looking at me.

"No," I answered surprised by his question. "How could you tell?"

"Didn't think ya did!" he said smiling.

We left Plate Creek at daybreak. Three black vultures with wings outstretched in a shallow-V soared above us rocking from side to side. We ate lunch next to a small mangrove island. The smell of my canned fish steaks on bread mingled with the odor of fish half eaten by turkey vultures. The food became tasteless. A family of bushy raccoons with dark eye masks stopped to watch our boat from the shore.

It took us five hours to paddle thirteen miles to reach the Rogers River Chickee. After setting up our tents we "bathed" by pouring the icy brackish water over ourselves with a jug. The cold water felt invigorating. Sheltered from the wind by thick mangroves, we sat cross-legged in the sun, studying our charts. A blue-gray belted kingfisher with a shaggy crest on its head swooped by cackling. It lit on a mangrove branch. With a sharp twittering call it dove into the water, snatched a fish with its beak, and returned to its perch to gobble it.

Life felt good, and I thought about how I could take risks when I felt in harmony with the universe. A four-mile winter solo canoe trip on Ichetucknee Springs River in Florida came to mind. With no one at the launch site, I had been unable to set up a shuttle to return to my car. Feeling strongly I would find a way back, I had started out anyway. "Do you need a ride to your car?" a man had asked before my canoe hit tne shore at the take out. I had graciously accepted.

At sunset the wind hit the water with a soft peaceful rippling sound. When the wind died, the bay became smooth and soft like a baby's skin. The mangroves looked black against the pink watery horizon. Venus twinkled just above the place where the sun had set.

"Pooh," came the gentle sound of a dolphin expelling air from its blow hole while it foraged across the bay. The Maoris of New Zealand regard the dolphin as a messenger from God. The dolphin's loving spirit is also reflected in the many stories about people who have been rescued by these intelligent, joyful beings. The dolphin's presence felt like a good omen.

Jay and I sat at opposite ends of the chickee admiring the stars, then we turned in for the night. Suddenly, I was awakened by a loud "crunching" sound next to my ear. I shone my flashlight around the tent, but saw nothing. My heart beat faster. "Did you hear that?" I asked Jay.

"No," he replied sleepily. Just as I put my head on the pillow, the "crunching" sounded again. This time it was a lot louder. My mouth went dry. Sitting up, I focused my flashlight's beam on my pillow. A two-inch ghost crab lifted and waved its claw pincers. Giggling with relief, I used my shoe to scoop it up and put it out.

Awakening, I glanced out the tent door. Giant snow-covered mountains filled the crimson sky. The jagged white peaks were mirrored in a pink glass-like lake. Was I in Nepal? Blinking in disbelief and panic, I looked again. The dazzling white mountains changed into huge billowing clouds. The sun's red orb glowed above the horizon of the bay's dome-like cathedral, creating an explosion of shimmering reds. I gasped in delight. A great blue heron soared across the sky and squawked as if to greet the fiery sun-god. Transformed by the deity of things, I felt like a pilgrim on sacred waters.

With no mosquitoes present, I left the door of my tent open. The tops of the clouds gleamed with a yellow white light before the sky became a web of pink and purple wispy clouds. A breeze turned the sun's reflection into tiny red ripples.

A gray six-foot alligator, with a broad snout, was sunning on the bank when we left Rogers River Chickee. Three brown pelicans passed in tight formation. The first left the line, flapped and glided across the water, then dove with a splash and scooped up a fish in its mandible. While floating, it tilted its head back to swallow the fish as water drained from its bill. Two dolphins made us laugh when they sped under the canoe's bow and rocked the boat.

Breezing down the Broad River with a northwesterly wind pushing from behind, we quickly covered nine miles. The brilliant sunshine seemed part of an eternal sacred ceremony.

Broad River, our next camp, was a ground site rated for twelve people. Three motor boats sped towards us and stopped. Seven men disembarked. "We left Chokoloskee this morning and we're here for two nights," said a gray-haired man. They were from West Palm Beach.

The camp ground became a beehive of activity, jokes and laughter while we set up our tents, but became silent when the men left to fish. Jay read a book while I sat on the wooden dock under a mangrove tree with thick green leaves. Our silence made Jay and me an odd couple, but I found myself growing fond of him.

The arched mangrove roots looked like a tapestry of spider webs. Volcano-like gray barnacles clung to the mangrove roots. Small snails with rough-banded white-and-black-pointed shells studded their trunks. Catching a whiff of gasoline from the twelve six-gallon red jugs that had been left on the dock by the fisherman, I was glad my canoe did not need fuel. The breeze's briny bath of air felt good on my skin and hair. An appreciation of all that was free filled me:

the sparkling mangrove wilderness, the ocean air, the brilliant sunshine and spectacular sunsets.

Long black snake-like necks of three anhingas surfaced in the water in front of me. One by one they disappeared and reappeared upstream. A small shore crab made its way down the trunk of a mangrove tree. It moved around the far side of the tree until only one stalk-like eye was visible.

Movies, books and television often mislead us by showing journeys into the wilderness involving horror, sickness, danger and death. What they leave out is the peace, the silence and the beauty.

I read with dismay about the history of the Everglades National Park. In the 1960s the Army Corps of Engineers shortened the Kissimmee River, which flows into Lake Okeechobee and the Everglades, from ninety-seven miles to fifty-four to provide water for cattle and sugar corporations. When the Everglades began to dry up and the water of southern Florida turned bad, they discovered that the Everglades had served as a giant filtering plant recharging its aquifer and cleansing the south-flowing water. When tourism, an industry ten times as big as sugar and cattle, dropped in the 1980s, restoration of the Kissimmee River and the Everglades was started. Problems remain. Agricultural development and the city of Miami continue to compete for water and space, and many of the animals remain endangered.

The fishermen returned at dusk and started a fire to grill steaks. "Would you like to join us for a fish dinner tomorrow night?" the gray-haired fisherman asked, looking at me.

"We may not have enough fish!" said another.

"There'll be enough for me and her!" he replied smiling. He looked at Jay, "Don't know about your friend." We all laughed.

Much to our surprise, the fishermen turned in early. Before going to sleep I thought about the next day. We would be canoeing the eight-and-a-half-mile Nightmare, a narrow creek that runs only at high tide. The name made me shudder. After Nightmare Creek, the trip would be halfway over.

CHAPTER 8

NIGHTMARE

God speaks to us within our thinking. God is within every flower and tree, animal and bird, crystal and cloud and ocean wave.

Sir George Trevelyn

Massive clouds clogged the sky obscuring the sun when we entered Nightmare Creek thirty minutes before low tide. The water looked to be four feet below the wet line on the mangrove trees, and there was a strong smell of sulfur. The tree leaves on both banks met overhead forming a green tunnel. Small gray birds peeped while flittering among the leaves. "I like the little, biddy birds," Jay commented. "They're so small you can't get a good look to see what they are."

A white snowy egret with bright yellow feet and a black bill foraged among the tree roots ahead of us in search of fish. "I didn't think we would get this far," I said after we had paddled a couple of miles.

"Yeah," Jay agreed. Two fallen trees blocked our channel around the next bend. "I'm going to lie back in the canoe to wait for the tide," Jay mumbled stretching out.

"I think we can get out on the logs and lift the boat," I suggested.

"I don't like it," Jay said eyeing the dead trees and mud.

"It could be fun, like an obstacle course," I said brightly. I got out gingerly, stood on the log and lifted the canoe bow across. Jay got out quickly and slipped. His shoes sank deep into the mud.

"These are my only pair of sneakers," he snarled, and gave me a scorching look. After negotiating both logs we paddled with renewed vigor. We passed marker twenty-three at the Broad Creek intersection around noon. According to the chart, Broad Creek flows to the ocean and would provide a longer alternate route to our next camp. We continued on Nightmare, the shorter route.

A howling wind hit us with furious force, making our jackets' hoods flap rapidly against our backs. The gusts came from the south, the direction we were going. Thirty minutes later the boat lodged in a trickle of water less than an inch deep and narrower than the canoe's width. Mosquitoes zoomed in.

"Humf," Jay muttered while spraying himself with bug repellent. "We would not have left camp till eleven if the decision had been mine!" he said coldly, then scowled.

"Why didn't you tell me?" I asked surprised. He lay back on the canoe and looked at the tree tops. Irritated, I studied the chart again. "Jay, should we take the alternate route?"

"I don't care," he grumbled poking his lips out. "You got us into this, you get us out!"

I sat a moment in awkward silence. "Let's have lunch," I suggested, starting to look for my food.

"I suppose so!" Jay murmured, reaching for an apple. He sat in the canoe covered with frowns. High tide would not be for another two hours. The wind streamed through our hair and clothes. Suddenly, I wanted to tinkle desperately, even though my liquid intake hadn't been much.

The water began to rise, and the canoe floated forward a few feet before it stopped. We sat a couple of minutes. The boat moved forward again. Poling three feet farther, we broke free into deep water. We passed marker twelve without problems.

"Hurrah! We made it through Nightmare," I cried slapping my paddle on the water. Jay smiled. Risk and fear seem to awaken my sleeping senses, strip me of pride and rip apart my habitual blinders.

We arrived at the Harney River Chickee two hours later and I made a mad dash for the toilet. Our camp was behind an island at the intersection of Nightmare Creek and Harney River. The wind blew sharply, roaring in our ears and creating foot-high waves and white caps on the water. Harney River's current was so swift, I decided to tie the canoe lines in four places.

My weather radio reported that twenty to twenty-five knot southeast winds were forecast for the next three days. This was bad news, for it meant canoeing into the raging wind. I was grateful that the winds were behind us the first half of the trip when we were inexperienced.

Jay leaned against a chickee post reading a book about birds. The wind hummed in my ears as I sat across from him. A small yellow bird landed on the canoe in front of Jay and gave a tiny "peep." "Jay, look at the bird!" I whispered, but it flew off.

"Come back, bird, so I can identify you!" Jay snorted.

Gray and white puffy clouds floated north while the wind danced across the water and shook the mangrove leaves. The tops of the tall mangrove trees on the opposite bank had turned red. We found out later that they were dying from the cold spell.

At dusk we heard the soft "pooh, pooh" sounds and light splashes of a dolphin foraging nearby. Time and space seemed to go warp as my sense of self expanded.

At sunrise we started our ten mile paddle to the Sharks River Chickee. The howling, demanding southeasterly wind was blowing with full fury. Increasing steadily from the wrong direction, the wind walloped our faces and made every inch of the five-and-a-half miles to Tarpon Bay a challenge. The gusts gushed up the river and snatched at our paddles and clothes. We rowed hour upon hour, against the buffeting wind. Making the trip a meditation—stroke-in, stroke-out—helped. My hands had become stiff and swollen from tendinitis, and my arms and fingers ached.

We stopped to rest and have lunch in the canoe at Tarpon Bay. A great blue heron stood in a "freeze" pose while fishing among the reeds. With a lightning strike it caught a fish and swallowed it head first. Honking sharply, the heron pulled in its neck and soared off with slow heavy wingbeats.

With the tide, wind and the current finally with us, we made good time on the Shark River. Two motor boats roared past our canoe, ignoring the "No Wake, Manatee" signs. "Don't speeding boats injure the manatee?" I asked one of the boat owners who had stopped to fish.

"Yes," the man said curtly, as if to say, "So what!"

The up to twelve-foot long, large, bulky manatee with a rounded tail and no rear flippers is endangered. Only a few hundred are left. The mothers hold their calves against their breasts to nurse and, like other mammals that live underwater, they must have air to breathe. I was struck by their gentle spirits when swimming with them in Florida.

Five huge houseboats roared by; the sound of their motors replaced the birdcalls and the gentle lapping of waves. The smell of fuel overpowered the salty odor of the water. None of the boats slowed down for the canoe.

We unloaded our gear at the Shark River Chickee and had our second shower. The water was too cold to enjoy, but we were clean again. The wind felt warm as I leaned against the chickee pillars in the sun. Small gray clouds streamed north. Except for an occasional "peep, peep" from a nearby osprey, the place was silent.

I heard that eagles and osprey use the same nests for many years and live longer than smaller birds. The osprey dives deep and works hard, while the eagle prefers shallower water for fishing.

The mangroves on the opposite bank swayed in the breeze, moving in unison like cabaret dancers. I turned in at sunset for large salt water mosquitoes had bitten through my thick army pants in spite of a generous application of insect repellent. A continuous "hum" from clouds of hovering mosquitoes made the place sound eerie.

A rhythmic, dripping sound woke me up at daybreak. Although it was light in my tent, the world outside was obscured by a gloomy white fog. We were nervous about getting lost when we left Shark River camp to navigate in the swirling ground fog. The veil of mist lifted an hour later to reveal a tranquil, shimmering Oyster Bay. The searing hot sun beat down from a cloudless sky while its fiery, blinding echo in the water burned my face even though I had sunscreen on.

Leaving the Wilderness Waterway, we paddled west and took a break at the Oyster Bay Chickee. A young couple from Pennsylvania were packing up. "We rented a canoe at Flamingo Ranger station and got stuck in a mud flat at Lake Ingram for three hours," murmured the man. "We were exhausted when we got to Big Sable Creek," the woman groaned.

"We canoe the Glades when we visit my parents in Florida," the man explained. "We're big bird watchers, and we've spotted over three hundred species here," he said proudly.

"I've been a bird watcher for ten years, and I added twenty species this trip," the woman added. She drew up her legs and tucked her feet underneath her.

The twenty-five-knot southeasterly wind whipped the water and the leaves of the trees into a frenzy. The violent gusts came from the direction we were going, making paddling difficult. With the wind and the current against us, we struggled to gain inches. About two miles from Joe River Chickee, our destination, a couple in a green canoe greeted us in German accents. They pulled ahead in Mud Bay, but we found them having lunch at our new camp. The man introduced himself as Hans and his wife's name was Marie.

"Where're you heading?" I asked, getting out my food.

"We're spending the night at South Joe Chickee and leaving the Everglades tomorrow," Hans explained in a German accent. He was from Germany and Marie was from Holland, but both had been in the States a long time.

"What do you do for a living?" I asked with interest.

"I'm a physicist and my wife is a travel agent," Hans said looking at Marie. They too, had put in at Everglades City, but a day ahead of us, on December 23, when there were gale force winds and below freezing temperatures. "It was so cold at Sweetwater Chickee that twenty minutes after our water had boiled it turned to ice," Hans said gravely.

When I commented on their empty-looking canoe, Marie showed us their dinner for the night. "We carefully measure and package our freeze dried and dehydrated food." Her tiny package held pizza and cheesecake. Impressed, we pointed to our large quantity of canned food. "We also brought firecrackers to celebrate New Year's Eve," Marie said smiling. Of course we're going to set the firecrackers off at eight instead of midnight." Like us, they went to bed at seven and slept twelve hours. When they left to complete their six-mile paddle to South Joe Chickee they gave us a bag of spaghetti, sauce, and herbs.

The Pennsylvania couple arrived for lunch. They told us more about the birds. "We run a national newsletter on how to attract purple martins by hanging up gourds," said the man. They also sold the gourds and were going to visit a woman in Wrens, Georgia, who was their supplier.

"I've had bad luck getting purple martins to live in my gourds," Jay confessed.

"You should have three or four holes in the gourd bottom for drainage and paint the gourd white to keep it cool," the man told Jay. "Also, hang them fairly close to the house away from trees." They explained that the glossy blue-black mosquito-eating purple martins have a strong homing instinct and are largely dependent on gourds supplied by people. Purple martins are the largest birds in the swallow family and have a slightly forked tail.

After the second couple left, we set up our tents on the cove platform, and I washed my hair in the choppy shallows. Soft white clouds lined the horizon. For dinner we made the European couple's spaghetti. We were in our tents at dusk on

New Year's Eve. Despite insect repellent, we had been bitten by the mosquitoes and gnats. I gazed through my tent's screen door. Reds and pinks from the sunset lit up the sky and water.

Gray mist swirled and eddied, clogging the air on the first day of 1990. A brilliantly-colored rainbow stretched across the fog-filled southern sky when we started the six-mile paddle on Joe River to the South Joe Chickee. The rainbow arch mirrored itself in the still water, creating a giant mystical eye. The sun burned off the fog and the heat and humidity drained our energy. After a two-hour paddle we arrived at our double chickee that stood in an open bay. We were relieved.

A plate of cheesecake wrapped in plastic was left near the toilet seat. The label read: "To the Georgia crew from Holland and Germany. Happy New Year!"

We set up our tents and then lazed in the sun. A couple in a motorized canoe stopped to stretch. "Using a motor is cheating," I said with a smile.

"We canoed the Everglades last year and got lost," the man exclaimed.

"We spent the night on a chickee without food and sleeping gear," the woman lamented. Although another cold front with rain was predicted they planned to motor to Oyster Bay Chickee for the night.

A green Mohawk canoe appeared after lunch. "We're your neighbors for tonight," declared John and Cindy, a young couple from Wisconsin.

"This is our third night," John said while unloading their canoe. "We stayed at North Cape Sable and got caught in the mud at low tide on the first day. It was tough dragging the canoe to deeper water."

The water slapped the chickee with a rhythmic "splish, splash," and the wind, our constant companion, hummed in our ears, making the mangrove leaves chatter. The morning fatigue had gone, leaving wonderful warm waves of calm.

Three black vultures rode the thermals while circling in the distance.

After dinner Jay got in the canoe to clean his plate. Leaning too far forward, he fell overboard. John left his dinner and ran over to help. Grabbing the water-logged Jay under his arms the two of us hauled him onto the platform.

"I've washed my dishes from the canoe so many times, I got careless," he said apologetically.

At sunset the wind rushed with new life whipping the bay into a frothy fury. With the mosquitoes absent, we sat outside to watch the stars. The chickee shuddered when the wind hit, while unseen hands seemingly lifted the platform off its pole supports.

When I went to bed, large swirling waves pounded the groaning chickee. Each time a violent gust of wind struck, my dome tent bent double, and my body stiffened. I was sure my shelter would be scooped up and dumped in the water with each blast. Recoiling in horror, I felt a constant need to urinate and my swollen fingers ached. Finally, I fell into a fitful sleep.

The icy wind had become a scouring roar, forming three-foot waves and white caps at first light. Wearing sweaters, jackets and hats, we started our final eleven-and-a-half-mile paddle to Flamingo Ranger Station. Nervous about canoeing into the shrieking wind and tide, we left early.

It took every ounce of will to paddle six miles east across Whitewater Bay's gigantic, frothy bay into the wall of wind. Turning south with the wind for the last five miles, we seem to fly across Coot Bay Pond and down Buttonwood Canal to the Flamingo Ranger Station. We arrived before lunch, set foot on land, and hugged for the first time.

Back in Georgia, my spirit remained in the vast breezy bays of the Everglades, where the light is brushed with brightness and with the sense of being part of something bigger than myself. Feeling the gentle caress of a breeze against my face and hair, I realized that my relationship with the wind, water and sun had deepened. They had become dear friends, even beloveds. No, more than that, the wind had become the breath of God.

Now, my thoughts turned to sailing on Mother Ocean's gigantic temple. For me, a sailboat is like a big canoe designed for living aboard, but it also has the capability of moving forward by harnessing the wind in its sails. Before setting sail, I planned to spend ten days solo backpacking in the Cohutta Wilderness in north Georgia and to do another spirit quest.

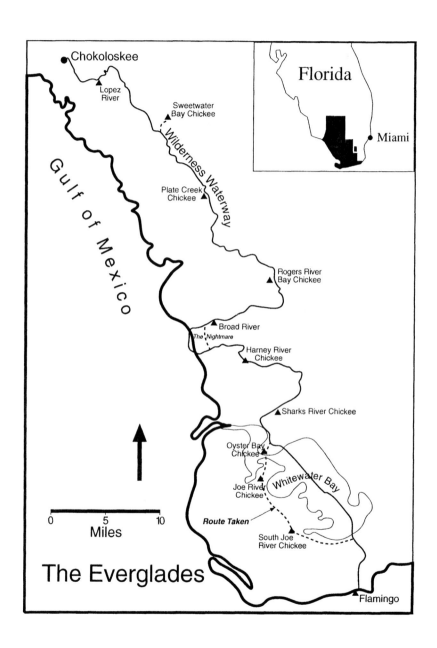

Chokoloskee

Lopez
River

Sweetwater
Bay Chickee

Wilderness Waterway

Gulf of Mexico

Plate Creek
Chickee

Rogers River
Bay Chickee

Broad River

The Nightmare

Harney River
Chickee

Sharks River Chickee

Oyster Bay
Chickee

Whitewater Bay

Joe River
Chickee

Route Taken

South Joe
River Chickee

Flamingo

Miles
0   5   10

The Everglades

Florida

Miami

CHAPTER 9

SOLO BACKPACKING

The earth does not belong to man; man belongs to the earth....Man did not weave the web of life, he is merely a strand in it. What he does to the web, he does to himself.

Chief Seattle

When I entered the Betty Gap trailhead on July 4, 1990 in Georgia's Cohutta Wilderness, I paused to look and breathe. Shadows loped along the mountains that filled the sky. Carrying my backpack home with me like a turtle, I felt an intoxicating sense of freedom. The mountains rang back the sound of my footfall as I stepped wide-eyed past the tall trees and the tiny rivulet that whirred downstream. Weightless with wonder, I prayed for guidance on my ten-day pilgrimage.

Sunlight shimmered on the thick, dark green leaves and the pale pink blossoms of the rhododendrons. The trail followed a rocky creek that tumbled down the mountain for two miles, then emptied into the larger fourteen-mile north-flowing Conasauga River.

Two women wearing small day packs walked towards me. "Beautiful trail," said the shorter woman in a soft, twitty voice. I agreed. Twenty minutes later a heavy-set man in a camouflage outfit strolled up carrying a fishing rod. He stopped, peered behind me and frowned.

"Ya hikin' alone?" he asked gruffly.

"Yes ... s!" I stammered, feeling uneasy.

"Ya so purty and men is men!" I smiled wearily and eased past him. "Ya'll take care now!" he waved.

After plodding a couple of miles into the wilderness, I pitched my tent among the flowering rhododendrons on a small flat area at the bottom of a mountain. Leaning against a tall tree near my tent, I sat mesmerized by the river scurrying across the rocks. Puffs of cool mountain air brushed against my face and played with my hair.

Outside of the Smoky Mountains, the Cohutta Wilderness is the largest mountain wilderness area in the East. Lying in the Southern Appalachian highlands, it extends north between Chatsworth and Ellijay, Georgia. The two distinct mountain ranges in North Georgia—the Cumberlands in the west and the Blue Ridge in the east—are separated by three regions of valleys and ridges. The sixty square miles of the Cohutta Wilderness is part of the western Blue Ridge and has round, flat-topped peaks covered with deep, damp, black soil.

The softer sandstone and limestone rocks of the flat mountains and boulders of the Cumberland Plateau have been carved for millions of years by the forces of nature. A vast tropical sea covered the area some six-hundred million years ago.

The Blue Ridge Plateau was formed about two hundred and thirty five million years ago, when the North American, European and African continents collided. As the rocks folded, through a movement called "plate tectonics", mountains and ridges formed and melted. Fast flowing rivers, wind and weather have worn as much as four miles off the mountains. The topsoil, the thin fragile covering of the rock, is forming at the rate of about one inch every fifty to a hundred years.

The name "Smoky Mountains" comes from the mild temperatures and heavy precipitation that makes the forest so dense that mist rises on warm days, often obscuring the mountain tops. Because the climate resembles that of New Jersey, North American birds such as the rose-breasted grosbeak and the scarlet tanager nest here.

Railroads, ties and trestles were built when seventy percent of the area was logged between 1915 and 1930, and their remnants can still be seen. Since 1600 the United States has lost ninety-five percent of its ancient forests. Because of technological advances hardwoods are now being used commercially along with soft woods. Alternatives such as recycled wood or kenaf, a twelve-foot woody plant rich in cellulose, are not considered because big companies lobby against it, and the timber and paper companies of the world are heavily subsidized by governments.

Traveling in the wilderness has become a trillion-dollar business and this money can be used to protect the earth's forests and wildlife sanctuaries. Some conservationists suggest the planet be seen as an Earth National Park or World Heritage and recommend putting boundaries around the cities, not around the wilderness.

Most of the fifteen trails in the Cohutta Wilderness follow the Jacks and Conasauga Rivers. The Jacks joins the Conasauga River on the Tennessee-Georgia border, then turns west and then south to become the Coosa River System. The guidebooks warn against hiking the Jacks or Conasauga River trails immediately after heavy rains, as the rivers rise rapidly and become dangerous to ford. Since we were experiencing a drought, these warnings did not concern me. With thirty-eight river crossings on the Conasauga, I hiked in rubber sandals and carried a pair of sneakers to use at night.

The sun was setting invisibly behind the mountains when I walked north for two miles. Possessed by racing thoughts, I marched, and missed my surroundings. Strolling back, I began to weep without knowing why. My pace slowed, and to my astonishment I felt great love for the trees, the river and the rocks as my senses came alive. Focusing on the murmur of the river's shallow riffles and the fading light, I prayed, "Please, Great Spirit help me and my earthly relatives to heal so we might save the planet and her disappearing wilderness."

Backpacking alone for ten days would be more challenging than my more structured canoe trips on the

Suwannee and in the Everglades. I planned to go where I was led and do a spirit quest when the time felt right.

When I went to bed, a strange blue-gray light spread through the forest. I woke in the night. My arms were numb, and I shivered from cold. Rearranging my "pillow" of clothes, I zipped up my sleeping bag and drifted off to sleep again.

A large lethal cobra snake lay on the path where I was walking with a female friend. The snake had dilated its neck like a hood. Seeing that its mantle was up I stopped, but my friend continued. To my horror, the cobra leapt and coiled itself around my throat. My friend tried get the snake off my neck by pulling at its thick body but could not free it. The snake pinched my throat when I tensed but did not hurt me when I relaxed. My heart beat wildly when I woke with a start, and was relieved to find that it had been a dream.

Thinking about the dream I decided the cobra was teaching me to stay calm in the midst of turmoil. Later I learned with interest that a cobra does not like to waste the venom it needs to incapacitate its prey and prefers to bluff an attacker with its startled eye-spots on the back of its hood.

Backpacking two miles north in the dewy cool of the morning, I pitched my tent in a cheery campsite next to chuckling ripples. The water must have leapt its banks earlier this year, I noted with a shiver, because limbs and sticks hung in the trees ten feet above the river bed.

Leaning on a walking stick for balance while day hiking, I stepped gingerly among the ankle-deep rocks at the first two river crossings. Feeling more confident at the third and fourth crossings, near the Panther Creek trail intersection, I waded swiftly by focusing on the feel of my feet on the rock ridges. Lying back on a boulder in the shade, I closed my eyes.

"Ka-ploosh, crack" came a sound behind me. Jumping up, I looked around. A fisherman wearing camouflage clothes was fly fishing in a backwater pool. He did not see me. Stretching out, I watched the white billowing clouds head east and the tree tops sway in tune with the bubbling water.

The fisherman's rod made a whipping sound while he worked his way towards me. Not wanting to startle him, I did not say anything. He moved closer and noticed me. "Hey," he said with a wave; then walked to my rock and sat down. He appeared to be in his fifties and wore a brownish baseball cap that said *Fireworks*.

"Catch anything?"

"Naw, didn't get them trout today," he said. He took out a cigarette with shaky hands. "Where ya from?" he asked glancing sideways at me.

"Macon, Georgia."

"I'm from Woodstock ... Canton area. Ya know it?"

"I've been through there."

"I'm camping with a buddy. Ya seen him?"

"No," I said nervously.

He got up, put out his cigarette and picked up his rod. "Ya be careful now," he said slipping back into the river.

Strolling back to my campsite, I saw the fisherman's friend fly fishing in a large pool. He jerked his head around, wide eyed. "You scared me there," he drawled. His hair was dark and he had a black mustache. I felt uneasy.

Back at the tent I leaned against a fir tree next to the creek. Sunshine filtered through the leaves of the swaying trees creating pools of light on the ground.

"Splash," came a sound from upriver. The fisherman with the mustache cast his fishing line while ambling towards me in the river. When he got to my tent, he stopped. "Brown trout are tough to catch," he said amiably. I nodded nervously. "A man caught a fifteen-inch brown trout yesterday," he stated with authority before disappearing down stream.

A sharp pain ran up the palm of my right hand. Jerking it up, I found that a striped yellow jacket bee had stung me. My palm hurt and became red and swollen. In pain I fidgeted and could not sit still.

When I went to bed a barred owl chortled its eight accented hoots in two groups of four above my tent. Its thrilling presence felt like a good omen.

After the sun had risen, flooding the forest with golden light, I broke camp and backpacked a half-mile downstream. A two-foot long reddish-brown snake with a fish the size of my hand in its mouth floated past in the current. The fish was alive and wiggled, but the snake held fast. They disappeared downstream.

A pink, flowery tunnel of rhododendrons shielded my new camp from the trail across the river. Two rotten trees with white fungi clinging to their bark lay collapsed and dead near my tent, their waste becoming humus for new growth.

I went for a stroll. Huge flat boulders sloped at an angle in the riverbend downstream. An overweight couple with backpacks stood at the Hickory Creek and Conasauga River trail intersection.

"Where're you hiking from?" I asked with interest.

"The lower Conasauga River trail," responded the man with a double chin.

"What's the trail like?"

"Much bigger, with huge gorges and deep pools," he said brightly.

"Sounds beautiful," I said intrigued.

"We've been out a week," the red-faced woman volunteered. "We started at Betty Gap, did the Panther Creek trail, Three Folks and some of the lower Conasauga."

"We're heading out tomorrow," the man added.

When I left the Hickory Creek trail for the lower Conasauga River trail the sun was high in the steely blue sky. The river ran through deep gorges where the water had cut its way through the mountains. Water leapt and splashed with a steady roar down the canyons into large pools fringed with ferns. Knocked breathless by the beauty, I raced ahead. I suddenly noticed there were no people and more opportunities to get hurt and became weary. After a couple of hours, I staggered back.

Back at camp, I soaked my tired body in the river. A six-inch brown speckled trout, with a transparent ventral fin, hovered within touching distance. I was stirred by the fish's trust. Its body seemed to be the home of the Holy One.

It felt right to start my spirit quest the next day. The moon hung fixed and full over the mountains, casting dappled shadows on the earth. Moonlight turned the shimmering water silver and threw the tall tree limbs into ghostly-looking sentinels. Tired, I went to bed.

Watching the faint promise of saffron in the east from my tent at dawn, I thought how some Native Americans believe it is good to quest during a full moon or when a woman is menstruating. Being more vulnerable, with high emotions and low defenses, she is said to be more in tune with nature and truth. I began my spirit quest at sunrise. The full moon and the starting of my period seemed like good omens.

I sat against a fir tree in the sun. A monarch butterfly with deep orange and black-rimmed wings flapped and circled. In flight, it looked like a leaf with a will. Hovering a moment, it landed on me. Astonished, I trembled in awe. Waving its hair-like antenna, it probed my skin with its delicate black proboscis and tiny feet. Could it really taste with its toes? When I moved, it vaulted off, then skittered and bobbed right back. Rolling up its proboscis, it slowly flapped its velvet mosaic-like wings covered with tiny scales. White dots shimmered on its small black head. Its slender brittle back had a shiny sheen. My spirit soared as I gazed at this tiny being. How strange that it had once been a woolly white, yellow and black caterpillar. When I stirred, it bounded up past the rhododendrons and out of sight. Having a butterfly for company had been an honor, and I felt lonely when it left.

100 Earth, the Forgotten Temple

Hot from the blazing sun, I moved in the shade, closer to the water. Large black ants tickled when they marched across my legs. I brushed them off. With practice I was able to ignore the black ants that walked on me except when they burrowed between my toes. Hunger and menstrual cramps made me feel weak and tired. While drinking water, I wondered how the Huichol Indians did vision quests without water.

As tree shadows lengthened and time passed half the river was in the shade. Facing upstream, I sat on a rocky seat still warm from the morning sun and touched the water with my bare toes. Brown, yellow and white pebbles rattled like dice.

Two backpackers staggered by; snatches of their blue and red packs flashed through the trees. Their loads seemed too heavy from the way they stumbled. Their presence unsettled me, for I envied their full stomachs, companionship and exercise. Feeling friendless, and hungry I was tempted to break my fast. I wanted to walk on the ridge behind the camp or swim in a pool downstream. I'd paid no money for the quest, and I answered only to myself and to Great Spirit; yet I abstained. My restraint filled me with confidence. Remembering how a beautiful butterfly had kept me company this morning, I felt comforted.

Voices seemed to whisper and shout above the gurgling water, but I saw no one. The day stretched on while the sun crept across the sky. My mind held vivid images of food. Feeling like forever, time extended on even after the river was mostly in shadow.

My thoughts turned to the story of our planet. Based on geological stratification and radioactive dating, scientists say that if the earth's history were compressed into a single year, the first eight months would be without life. Viruses, single-celled bacteria and jellyfish would appear in September. Mammals would emerge the second week in December and dinosaurs on Christmas Eve. Humankind would originate fifteen minutes before midnight on December 31. It was humbling to think that all of recorded history occupies only the last sixty seconds of December 31. My hunger returned me to the present.

This will be a one-day quest, I decided. The previous day I had been content; today I was hungry, lonely and bored. Turning my loneliness and hunger over to Great Spirit, I prayed. "Thank you for your many blessings. For the good earth and the sun and the food they provide. Also, for the earth's beauty that nourishes our souls. Creator, I pray for the healing of all my brothers and sisters, that we become healers, not destroyers. Please help us to put aside our wills so we can better serve you." Crying to Great Spirit for healing, I asked for forgiveness from others. My arrogance kept me angry; and I hoped that in forgiving I was forgiven.

The day felt like a lifetime. A spirit quest was humbling and felt much like choosing to get sick. Feeling tired, cold and hungry, I washed my face, hands and feet, brushed my teeth and went to bed. It did not take long to fall asleep.

My strength returned when I broke my fast at dawn. The sun's rays glowed through the forest to form pools of light on the gurgling river. I went for a stroll. The steeple-like trees sparkled in the sunshine and the air was thick with the scent of lichens, mosses and mushrooms. Feeling radiant and alive like a flower strewn field, I hummed to myself. There were four river crossings before the Panther Creek trail turn-off.

At the third crossing there was a scramble of wild confusion when a doe took off across the river, its white tail high like a flag. Her brown, spotted fawn stood motionless behind a bush. Kneeling spellbound, I crept closer to get a better look. The white spots on the fawn's golden back shimmered through the shrubs. Then with a rush, the fawn raced towards me and with a mighty bound veered off and landed behind a bush a few paces from me.

Ashamed of keeping the mother from her baby, I crossed the river and squatted against a rock. The trembling fawn darted to the river's edge farther upstream. Looking over its shoulder, it listened intently and then whirled around and slipped behind a rock. Suddenly, the doe daintily stepped into the river and the fawn dashed to her side. Facing me, they stood together, their golden brown bodies and eyes shining in the misty yellow-white light. A waterfall surrounded by pink rhododendron flowers thundered in the background. I smiled with pure pleasure. Then they were gone.

Another brown long-legged doe entered the river as I was about to leave. She strolled forward, stopped at the waterfall and cupped her pointed ears. Stunned that the deer could stand before me unfrightened, I sat frozen. It seemed like a scene in paradise in which some spell held me. Then with a flick of her white tail, she vanished. Placing the picture of the deer in my gallery of memories, I skipped down the trail.

A dark-haired, blue-eyed, bearded man stood at the Conasauga and Hickory Creek trail intersection. A rush of energy told me something important was about to happen. My heart beat faster. "Hi," I greeted him. "Where are you heading?"

"Towards Betty Gap," he said. His blue eyes held my gaze.

"Where did you come from?" I asked eyeing the large gray pack on his back.

"Tearbritches. I'm doing a loop." He smiled. "Have you been there?"

"No ... I hear it's hard."

"Tell me about it!" He laughed. "I'm Wayne Ozier," he said extending his hand and giving a firm handshake.

"Where are you from?" he asked adjusting his backpack.

"Macon; and you?"

"Atlanta; I used to live in Macon once, and hated it."

"Oh, why?"

"A number of things ... the job, my supervisor, where I lived, the people."

"What were you doing?"

"Vocational Rehabilitation. I'm out of the field now. I work for the I.R.S."

"That's a big change!" I chuckled.

We realized we had a lot in common. An hour later we had covered the gamut—our histories, philosophies, values, hopes, dreams, and our different religious and spiritual views. He was an atheist.

"I've never exchanged this much information with a person in so short a time," I said smiling.

"Me neither; let's keep in touch," he said, taking my phone number and waving good-bye. Feeling a warmth about my heart, I hoped I'd see him again.

When I turned to leave two men and three boys with backpacks walked up. "You're standing on a turtle hatchery," exclaimed a man in a blue plaid shirt. He pointed to my feet. Looking down I saw a nest of empty broken eggshells.

"Wow," I said surprised.

"The eggs have been eaten, probably by raccoons," the man continued.

"We saw two wild pigs last night," volunteered a freckle-faced boy.

While hiking to the lower Conasauga River trail, I thought about North America's fifty species of toothless, beaked, bony-shelled turtles. I had fond memories of seeing these cold-blooded reptiles basking in the sun on logs in the river to raise their temperature and speed up their metabolism.

The water at the top of a cliff poured down a thirty-foot drop into a big clear pool fringed by green ferns and a clean white beach. The beach was backed by a steep rock face. Determined to get to the white sand, I hiked down the opposite bank and swam across the pool. Three large potatoes, two onions and a handful of mushrooms lay on a rock. Picturing potatoes and onions in my broccoli soup, I scooped them up and put them in my daypack.

My encounters with Wayne and the deer and the discovery of fresh produce seemed like gifts from Great Spirit. After a swim, I drip dried among the rocks in the sun. I thought about Wayne's comment that not everyone can hike alone. A friend of his was stung by fifty yellow jacket bees within an hour of his first solo attempt at backpacking. When he bent to pick up his stick, he was startled by a rattlesnake coiled to strike. Terrified and in pain, he hiked out, drove home and never went alone again. The man in the plaid shirt said he had seen two poisonous snakes that morning and nearly stepped on the copperhead. The universe was strange; it seemed to have treated me so well while subjecting others to hazards.

Dark clouds gathered and thunder rumbled in the distance. I looked up. The sky became a burst of light, revealing black, rolling clouds. The crackling crash of thunder was so loud I feared it would shatter and split the cliffs. Then came a few stinging drops. To be safe from lightning I considered my options: the woods, a rock in the middle of the river, or a ledge at the base of two tall trees. The ledge was the most dangerous, but since it gave the best view of the storm, that's where I went.

Lightning bolts lit up the world a few seconds before a booming thunder clap echoed through the mountains. A cold, driving rain blotted out the canyon. Although my poncho kept me dry, the crashing thunder next to my head and the roar of the river rising left me dazed. Jumping up, I traipsed back in the beating rain.

Thinking the odds of being struck by lightning was equivalent to winning the lottery, I later learned was foolish. The voltage from a lightning strike can jump or radiate through the ground, metal or water to affect a large area. Seventy percent of people survive a down strike, but none survive the earth's up to fifty thousand degree Fahrenheit upward strike. Strikes originating in the clouds dissipate in the air so that the actual strike contains only a few thousand volts.

The sun came out a couple of miles from my tent light and the veils of mist melted in the clean pure air. Back at camp, I started dinner. The onions smelled delicious and I was salivating. After a hearty meal of potato and broccoli soup, I went for a walk upstream in the fading light. A haze hung in the air and there was an occasional rumble of thunder in the distance.

A man and a girl were throwing pebbles in a pool at the second river crossing. "Are you camping?" I asked, noticing two backpacks propped against a tree.

The man threw another stone. "Yes. We don't know where ... somewhere," he said without looking up. The girl, who seemed to be around ten, threw another pebble.

Her pebble bounced repeatedly across the water. "I won, Daddy!" she shrieked with delight. Her father smiled.

Something ahead disappeared behind a tree stump at the next river crossing. Rounding the stump, I froze. A grayish-brown white-tailed doe and her tiny golden-spotted fawn were standing in shallow riffles. Stunned, our eyes fixed on each other. There was a whirlwind of racing hooves as the doe took off, almost knocking down her fawn. The fawn stood motionless before me looking bewildered and dazed. Then it leaped in the air and bounded off. My heart beat faster. For five days I'd not seen deer. Then the day after my spirit quest, I saw five. Hallowed by their presence, I felt connected to the universal current of life.

When I returned to camp the rhododendron's leaves, wet from the rain, looked sparkling clean. A gentle mist hovered above the water before the river slowly faded into darkness.

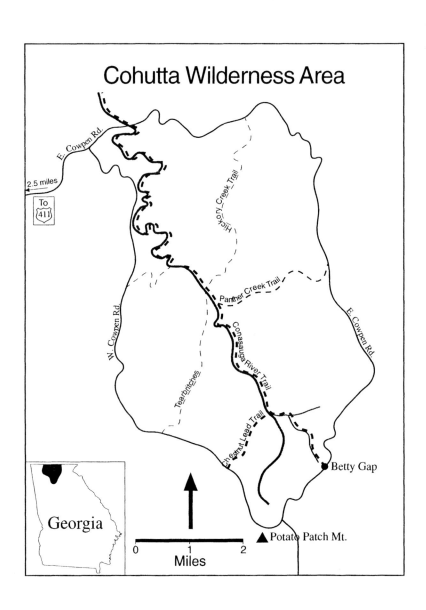

Cohutta Wilderness Area

E. Cowpen Rd.

2.5 miles

To 411

Hickory Creek Trail

Panther Creek Trail

W. Cowpen Rd.

Conasauga River Trail

E. Cowpen Rd.

Tearbritches

Chestnut Lead Trail

Betty Gap

Georgia

Potato Patch Mt.

0   1   2

Miles

CHAPTER 10

LETTING GO

One touch of nature makes the whole world kin.
William Shakespeare

We are part of the earth and it is part of us. Love the earth as the new-born loves its mother's heartbeat.
Chief Seattle

It was time to move on. Not knowing what I would do each day felt strange; yet a clear plan emerged the following morning. Perhaps the canyon had something to teach me. I set up my tent next to the trail on top of the mountain near the waterfall. While eating the last of my potato and broccoli soup for lunch, I considered how wearing a heavy pack distracted me from the wild. My focus was not on my surroundings but on keeping my balance, the discomfort from the pack's weight, and getting to my destination.

The pool below the waterfall was so big I could swim around and watch the minnows nip and scatter around my skin. The hot rocks became an armchair when I sun-dried near the thundering falls.

A thin veil of mist crept across the sky while I was hiking downriver. Enjoying the adventure of being in new territory, I pushed ahead. The trail wound over steep cliffs, and criss-crossed down huge canyons and waterfalls. The pungent smell of fir and pine trees hung in the air. July was a good time to ford the river because the water level was low. Wayne told me he had waded through waist-deep water on more than one occasion in the spring. Hearing the sound of rustling leaves, I stopped.

A long-legged brown doe stood frozen among the rocks on the hillside. She turned her eyes and ears towards me in easy confidence. Spellbound, I stood gaping. Her legs shivered and her stomach muscles twitched. Moving her head up and down she snorted, turned her black snout to the side and sniffed. Then she whirled around and ran uphill. Sneezing a couple of times, she stopped, gazed at me through her soft mournful brown eyes, then vanished into a serrated row of pines. I retraced my steps, filled with the staggering glory of being alive.

Three sheets of clear plastic had been left in a neighboring camp. Rolling them up, I placed two behind a tree and took the third to use as a ground cloth for sleeping out that night. I returned to camp. The skies darkened and it began to thunder. A blinding lightning bolt lit up the canyon, and the world became one huge boom. Its volume shook the ground. The heavens opened, pouring rain like a waterfall.

I sprinted to my tent and found that pools of water had collected inside. Adjusting the fly lines helped. The thunderclaps and lightning flashes came close together. Feeling nervous, I was glad to be distracted with water-proofing my tent. The drumming of raindrops on my tent fly competed with the reverberating thunder booms and the flickering lightning. The skies grew even darker. Thunder, lightning and heavy rain continued for over an hour. Cold and wet, I changed into dry clothes and ate trail-mix for dinner. When the rain stopped the waterfall's roar sounded louder.

I looked out my tent and my mouth went dry. The fast-flowing current, brown with mud, had risen over a foot and was swift enough to sweep a person into the gorge. Fortunately the rains had come after I returned from my hike. If an hour of rain could cause the river to rise so rapidly, more rain would be extremely treacherous.

I hiked to the river crossing upstream to see if I should leave. The river was slightly higher but clear. A swollen creek entering the Conasauga on the opposite shore was responsible for the flood downstream. Relieved, I sat on a rock to enjoy the raging creek.

When I returned to the canyon I used the plastic groundcloth to make a rain shelter over my tent by covering a V-shaped tree limb. Then I strolled over to the river to wash my face. The thundering sound of the water felt disturbing. I jerked my hand back in alarm. A red-and-brown-striped snake had hidden in a rock crevice I was about to use. I looked more closely. I thought it was a cottonmouth, but it did not have the vertical pupils and the wedge-shaped head of a poisonous snake. My heart beat faster. I tried to recall what I knew about venomous snakes in North America.

I'm told that cottonmouths, like copperheads and rattlesnakes, are pit vipers. Between each eye and nostril is a deep temperature sensitive receptor that allows it to detect warm-blooded prey. They have two long hollow venom-injecting fangs, and unlike other snakes give birth to live young, which are venomous at birth. I learned later, to my surprise, that the cottonmouth is not found in north Georgia.

The slow darkness, the raging water and the snake lit a flame of terror that began to burn bright. The gorge seemed to be a place of power with its roaring waterfall, walls of stone, huge boulders and terrific thunderstorms.

Crawling into the tent, I turned my fears over to Great Spirit. Repeating, "Let go, let God" in my head, I thought how the universe had taken care of me in the past. Knowing I was seven miles from my car and three miles from an empty parking lot did not help. Frightened by God's powerful Spirit in nature, I continued to pray. Sleep would not come.

People seemed to be singing. I bolted upright to listen. Some folks laughed and cheered; others whooped and hollered. My heart beat faster. Were there other campers or was I hallucinating? Someone began to play a harpsichord in what sounded like a pub. My mouth went dry. Surely I was alone. Had the clamor of civilization followed me in my head or could there be audible electrical waves in the air? I began to shiver. I lay motionless with my head against the pillow. The sounds got more boisterous. I half rose. The song of a church choir overpowered the waterfall's roar. My skin turned to gooseflesh. Trembling with exhaustion and terror, I fell asleep.

When I looked out my tent on Tuesday morning the sky was pink. A baby was crying while people sang hymns. My pulse quickened. I looked around, but there were no other campers. The songs of civilization were definitely coming from within and around me but my fear had disappeared with the darkness. Awed by life's mysteries, I named the place "Vision Mountain" for its teachings seemed to be about the songs of humankind, power and fear.

While combing my hair I noticed that my right eye was very red. Looking closer, I found a small gnat. So far, two bugs had committed suicide in this eye. The sky started out hazy, but rays of sun broke free, lighting the tree-tops and forming dappled shadows on the ground. Everything was wet from the rain the night before, and a strong scent of soil, moss and decaying leaves was evident. The Conasauga River's water level was normal, so I stepped down the trail to the sound of orchestral music.

When I entered new territory my anxiety rose. Walking slowly, I hoped to see deer. A three-person blue dome tent was pitched on the trail. Assuming the occupants were asleep, I moved silently. After hiking a couple of hours I turned back.

Two men in their twenties sat on stools in front of their tent. They gaped at me. "Where're you heading?" I asked.

"Downstream," said the man wearing a red T-shirt. They had parked at the Hickory Trail entrance and were in for three days.

Near the next river crossing a smooth, slim-bodied, foot-long eastern ribbon snake was draped on a bush. Three bright yellow stripes ran down the length of its dark body which molts several times a year. Kneeling, I crept closer to get a better look. The snake slid behind a small twig. Its face and round, unwinking eyes looked like a lizard's. When I stirred, it coiled back its head and flickered its forked tongue. Feeling guilty about frightening it, I started back. Back in camp, I hung my wet clothes in the sun to dry and estimated I'd hiked eight miles.

I tried to relax on a ledge above the waterfall but rock music filled the air. My head began to hurt from the noise and the waterfall's roar made it worse. When a nap on the rocks did not help, I took two aspirin and had dinner upstream, where the music and water sounded quieter.

Dark clouds formed and thunder rumbled in the distance. The gloomy black clouds became more solid. Lightning flashed and thunder boomed. After the first rain drops, I moved under the trees, but the rain poured through their branches. Dazed, I ran to my tent and sat leaning against a tree under the plastic canopy. When the rain subsided after an hour, my head had cleared. Checking both river crossings, I found the creek had swollen, but nothing like the day before. Praying out loud before going to bed brought me peace. The songs of civilization were there, but they did not keep me awake.

When I woke at daybreak a nightmare was still fresh. I was having dinner with my father and Dorothy, my stepmother. Two huge blocks of cheese were on the table. My father gave me a slice. "You did not prepare for my visit," I said tearfully.

"She's right," Dorothy said scowling at my father. When I woke more completely, I felt angry about being abandoned in my childhood. In my mind I held court, and cross-examined my father.

"Nicholas LaRocca, how many children do you have?" asked the prosecuting attorney.

"One."

"Is Niki Collins your daughter?

"Yes."

"How much child support did you pay?"

"None."

"How many times did you see her as a child?"

"None."

"Did you know she was in an orphanage as a child?"

"No."

"Could you have visited her?"

"Yes."

"Who made the first contact?"

"My daughter."

"How many times have you visited your daughter in the last eighteen years?"

"Twice."

"How many times has she visited you?"

"I've lost count."

I cried for the little girl who did not get what she needed from her parents. There was no need to put my mother on the witness stand; I'd already tried and convicted her. I wanted to put the past behind me. I was forty years old and had done enough grieving. I loved my parents and knew they did the best they could. Tears of forgiveness flowed like the river, soaking my face and clothes. I hoped my parents had it in their hearts to forgive me also for any hurt I may have caused them.

When I opened my tent, the first glow of light was on the horizon, and cool air entered. The trees looked serene in the semi-darkness. Everything was wet from last night's rain, and there was a smell of earth.

"Crack!" A sound like a pistol shot reverberated through the woods. I jumped in fright and scambled out my tent. A tree had crashed to the ground in the vicinity of my bathroom. There was no breeze. The limb that fell, came from a tree with two trunks the same size. The fallen limb looked waterlogged.

The songs of civilization had become more "primitive," sounding like African and Native American chanting. They were softer and more joyful. It was easy to tune into the songs, but I had to make a conscious effort to listen to the river.

Sunlight danced on the water when I laid my gear out to dry. Because I was content, the waterfall sounded gentler. Strange how the noise in my head colored the world. With only two days left, it was time to camp closer to my car. Taking down my tent, I backpacked to the Panther Creek and Conasauga River trail intersection.

I washed my plate after lunch. A dark brown, two inch long, dusky salamander lay among the rocks. I moved closer but it withdrew behind a stone. Dropping to the ground, I held my breath. Its wet, blotchy body reappeared half walking, half swimming among the pebbles. Inching closer, it lifted its lizard-like head out of the water, pumped its throat rapidly to increase air flow, and placed it on a stone. Two big soft round child-like eyes watched me. Sitting stone-like, I felt as if I was seeing the salamander for the first time.

A salamander's world is different from ours. It hears nothing and makes no sound. Lacking gills and lungs as adults, salamanders breathe through their skins and the lining of their mouths. The salamander's grape-like clusters of eggs are laid in soft soil and the newly hatched larvae live on land before entering the water.

A yellow jacket landed on my foot. When I brushed it off, the salamander moved to the bottom of the pool and vanished. For company I had a salamander, a hand full of water bugs, and a yellow jacket. Yet, I was content. When I stopped thinking my awareness seem to intensify. Had I lost my sensitivity to develop my intellect? Losing my mind to come to my senses felt stunning.

Three men in uniforms with backpacks strolled up. They looked like forest rangers.

"Hi," said the gray-haired man, taking off his pack. "You by yourself?" he asked looking around.

"Yes. Are you from the Forest Service?" I asked to confirm my suspicions.

"Yes. We're on a trash run," the younger man said pointing to his pack. All their backpacks looked full. They put their packs down.

"Where're you from?" the gray-haired man asked.

"Macon, Georgia. How about you?"

"Ellijay," he said smiling.

"Did you come in at Betty Gap?" I asked.

"Yes; why?"

"Did you see a white Hyundai?"

"No," said the gray-haired man thoughtfully. My heart beat faster until I noticed the other rangers grinning.

"Don't tell her that!" said the younger ranger. Relieved, I began to relax.

"How long have you been in here?" the older man asked.

"Eight days." He looked surprised.

"When you leaving?" asked the younger ranger.

"Friday ... today's Wednesday, isn't it?"

"You've been in here too long if you're losing days," the gray-haired man said laughing.

"I like it that way!" I chuckled. They left smiling.

Before leaving, the rangers said two women were camping at the Chestnut Lead trail entrance. Since they were having breakfast the rangers had not stopped to talk. Two flies landed on my arm. Remembering that all life is holy, I blew them off. My blowing on them felt more peaceful.

A flat area under some trees near a quiet deep pool became my next campsite. To get to the site I had to leave the trail and cross the river. Before putting up my tent I looked for hazardous tree limbs. A fallen tree made an archway over my tent.

A yellow jacket was trapped in the water between two rocks. Floating on its wings, it struggled at first and then became still. Thinking of the many times I had been stung, I resisted rescuing it. But since I was practicing unconditional love, I picked it up and placed it on a stone. Instead of taking flight when saved, it fell into the water again. The current swept its body into a pool, where a fish bit at its head. I rescued it again. It walked around and then took off.

It began to thunder and sprinkle. "Boom" came the thunder with lightning flashing across the sky. Since it was close to dark, I got inside my tent. The rain intensified and drummed against my rain fly. There was nowhere to hide; I was already in a valley and surrounded by trees. It drizzled through the night. When the rain stopped at dawn a rhythmic drip punctuated the silence. The river had risen slightly but was clear.

Sitting in the tent doorway, I thought how cities seemed boring compared to the wilderness; there was so much more to see and do in the wild. It seemed to me that our busy schedules and the trappings of modern society isolate us from nature, and leave little time for the stirrings in our souls. We express our suffering through increased isolation, addictions and violence and by allowing the earth's air and water to be poisoned.

Living in the woods and in the moment, the distinction between my inner and outer world disappeared. I felt a part of all beings, all creation. I looked in the mirror to comb my hair. My face appeared more peaceful than I had ever seen it, and my body, though stiff in places, felt stronger and healthier.

Blue sky became visible between the white, fluffy, transparent clouds that floated east. Everything was wet, green and clean-looking. A mottled, misty light shone through the leaves, creating pools of sunlight on the trees.

I backpacked to the next campsite. The clouds grew thick and dark. Thunder rumbled and a soft rain began. To keep my gear dry I put a cover over my backpack. Leaving the trail, I crossed the river to my first night's campsite, the small flat clearing at the base of a mountain. I was back where I first started but the journey had changed me. The place seemed different; my love for the woods had grown, and being with the trees felt as comfortable as my home.

After putting up my tent I looked for the women the rangers had mentioned, but they had gone. A freshly dug trench gaped where a tent had been. On a rock stood a large red apple. Presuming it a gift, I washed and ate the apple. Thinking about Eve in the Bible, it occurred to me that it was our destiny to eat of the fruit from the tree of knowledge. How else could we have begun the journey of spiritual discovery?

A side trail water cascaded down three, two-foot drops into a deep pool. Sitting cross-legged next to the pool, I felt a sense of peace and power. The world became dark when more clouds gathered. Hiking back, I crossed the river and returned to my tent.

The songs of civilization were still with me. All the inhabitants of the earth were represented—Native American, East Indian, Asian, African and European. A rooster even crowed periodically. I'd heard of the song of the universe and remembered with delight that "uni-verse" means "one song." Since I liked the singing, I did not mind. It began to rain and I moved inside my tent. At first there was a pitter-patter, then the drops got larger and the drumming started. The rain continued for over an hour.

"A flood!" I cried. The river's tinkle had turned into a roar. I peered at the boiling river with a flashlight. My mouth went dry. The surging water had turned brown and looked too high and too fast to cross safely. My hands shook. I was trapped at the bottom of a mountain only four feet above the thundering water. I looked at my watch. It was nine. I frantically considered my options. If I climbed the steep slope there was nowhere to pitch my tent. Staying in my tent seemed best; at least I was dry. Too scared to sleep, I kept checking the water level. The rain on the tent sounded like hail, and every drop meant the river would get bigger. By midnight, the boiling water was still rising. My heart began to pound. If the river rose two more feet I'd be washed away. Trembling with fear, I thought of crossing the river to be done with the terror, but in the dark and in a state of panic it would not be safe. Two hours later the river's snarling waves still thundered like a waterfall smashing against the rocks.

Then a miracle! The rains slacked off and stopped. Exhausted, I fell asleep. I woke with a start at five when the rain's pitter-patter became a roar. Squinting into the blackness with my flashlight, I gasped. The rushing river was down a couple of feet, but it was still too dark to cross safely. The rain's drumming on the tent reminded me the that river could rise again.

The rain slacked off around six. I jumped out of my tent and broke camp in the semi-darkness. The faster I worked, the more mistakes I made. My Therm-a-Rest mattress refused to roll up, my sleeping bag got stuffed into the wet tent bag, and I became tangled in the tent ropes.

I was finally packed. A brooding gray sky framed the overcast day. My eyes focused on the white waves that leaped and whirled, spraying the air. Shivering, I plunged into the swift current. The brown water swirled around my legs, wetting the bottom of my shorts. Waves punched and slapped my thighs, forcing me down stream. Pushing back against the wall of water, I inched forward, fighting to keep my balance. My feet felt like lead in the surging current. Shaking from exhaustion and fear and more aware of the preciousness of life, I collapsed on the opposite bank and gave Great Spirit a heartfelt "thank you."

Then I slowly began the two-mile, relentlessly steep thousand-foot ascent to my car at Betty Gap. An eerie mist shrouded the trees enclasped by ferns and lichen. The trees, the leathery vines and the plants seemed woven into each other. The smell of leaves was evident. When my heart raced, I stopped to rest. A gentle rain cooled my sweaty body.

Scurrying out of the trail, I changed into dry clothes. And then I began my slow descent down the mountain in my car. The rain strengthened, making deep channels in the gravel, and the air hung thick with mist. My body remained tense until I came to the paved road.

Something did not feel right. All I could hear was the hum of the car engine, the dancing windshield wipers and the pitter-patter of rain. The song of the universe had gone! I felt a great loss.

Four months later, after a number of phone calls and wilderness trips together, Wayne quit working for the I.R.S. in Atlanta and started working as a social worker in Macon. We had become good friends.

The ten days alone in the wilderness had far reaching effects—it made me want to simplify my life. My pace became slower, I sought softer music and I drove my car at a more leisurely speed. My desire for more possessions decreased, and shopping malls and other crowded places felt oppressive. As my creativity expanded, I felt less inclined to escape into movies, books and television. Most of all, I had a greater appreciation for the divinity of all things.

A year later I returned to "Vision Mountain." If I'd known I would nearly be murdered, I would never have gone.

As acting director for our Mental Health Center's children's program, I was unsure whether I wanted to take the position on a permanent basis. Taking time to meditate and pray while alone in the wilderness seemed like a good way to get answers. Backpacking four miles along the Conasauga River's rich carpet of luxurious forest, I set up my tent among the rhododendrons near the water.

The following morning, I started hiking the three miles to my favorite waterfall. Sunlight shone through the tree tops. Usually, I walk slowly, pausing to take in the sights, sounds and smells of the trail, but being preoccupied, I experienced little.

As I approached the mountain the roar of the waterfall announced its presence. I became nervous for I had an odd feeling something was about to happen but ignored it. Hopping from rock to rock, I crossed the river above the falls and sat cross-legged against a tree on a ledge. Gazing at the water as it plunged down a steep ridge, I tried to relax, but my heart was too burdened for peace.

A dark-haired, heavy-set, bearded man with a fishing rod lurched and stumbled on the rocks below before vanishing in the woods. I looked up and chills went up my spine. The bearded man stood across the river from me, urinating in full view. He swayed and leered at me with a twisted half-smile on his lips. Embarrassed, I looked downstream until he had gone.

Getting up to leave, I glanced towards the falls. My heart began to pound. The bearded man was staggering towards the river crossing below me. His eyes were locked on me. In his hand was a machete. I gaped in stunned silence. Etched on his glowering lips was the twisted half-smile. My mouth went dry. The man looked dangerous. I frantically considered my options. There was little chance of seeking aid on the remote down-river trail, but I'd seen campers on my way to the falls; if only I could slip by the man.

Feigning calmness, I crossed the river and strode towards him. My heart hammered and my legs felt like lead. *My life's over*, I thought with a shiver. When I drew near he jumped reflexively. And then he stuck his chin out and pointed the machete at my throat. I stared at the machete, my eyes transfixed with horror. Then my blood surged and I gave him a scorching look. "What's that for?" I barked, surprised at my ferocity.

His head snapped back and his lips curled in disgust. "Firewood," he slurred, waving the machete at me scornfully. Our eyes met. His were not quite focused and looked crazed. I jerked away and darted passed him.

"Shit! Wait!" he muttered following me.

I drew in my breath and yelled, "Have a good day!"

Don't run! I thought in a wave of terror. *You'll provoke him.*

"Wait!" he hissed from just behind me. I refused to look back. Ignoring my heart's runaway throbbing, I splashed across the river towards the trail intersection.

"Kaploosh!" I heard him fall. "Shit!" he snorted. My heart thumped against my ribs. I reached the bank, but I could hear his footfalls close behind me. My heart fluttered in my chest as I tried to catch my breath. Sweat poured down my armpits.

Then miraculously, from out of nowhere, three men on horseback trotted up. Falling in step with the last horse, I stumbled after them. We rounded a bend. Turning to the last tall, stern-looking rider, I blurted, "You've saved my life!" in a voice shrill with panic. Tears spilled down my face.

"You okay?" the man muttered briskly, getting off his horse. I nodded, brushing the sweat from my hairline with trembling hands. The other men stopped.

"What's wrong?" asked the short lead man. Still shivering, I told them what happened.

"We saw you with the man," said the lead man, shaking his head. We thought you were together.

"Do you carry a gun?" asked the tall man.

"No," I said weakly.

"You should," said the lead man, sounding irritated. Satisfied that I was unharmed, they mounted their horses and moved on.

Fearing the bearded man would follow, I kept looking over my shoulder. It was past lunch time, but I was not hungry. Hot and exhausted, I collapsed upriver, away from the trail to rest. Loneliness and desolation swam inside me. Closing my eyes, I prayed. I looked up and blinked furiously. A couple was crossing the river downstream. Tears came to my eyes. If only I could talk to them. They stopped on the opposite bank. *Wish they'd come over!* my heart cried. Seeing me, they waved and left. I felt a great loss.

Moments later a wide-eyed woman wearing a blue western-style shirt walked up. "My husband and I felt you needed to talk to us," she said gently.

I sat bolt upright. "Yes!" I wept, my skin turning to gooseflesh. She put her arms around my shoulders and held me while my story poured out. Her athletic-looking, sandy-haired husband strolled up and began boiling water for tea. They introduced themselves as Lynn and Virgil.

"You were too far away for us to see your face, but somehow we knew something was wrong," Virgil said crisply.

"We tried to leave, but the feeling was so strong," Lynn said in amazement. "We both felt it."

"Reacting unpredictably saved your life," Virgil announced, when he heard my story. He looked at me keenly through hawk-like eyes.

"Yeah, you didn't act like a victim," Lynn explained.

Soon we were laughing and joking. To our delight we discovered that all three of us not only experienced God's love through nature but we also shared an interest in Native American spirituality.

"What do you do for a living?" I asked, sipping my peppermint tea.

Virgil looked embarrassed. "I teach people how to kill! I'm in the army," he said studying the ground. "It's time to get out."

"I'm a nurse," Lynn said, interlacing her fingers around her knees. "Would you like us to camp with you tonight?" she asked peering at me.

"Yes!" I sputtered with my heart in my throat. "I thought I'd have to go home."

We parted the following day and exchanged addresses. "You're truly earth angels," I told them. Driving home trembling in awe, I knew what I wanted to do. I would not only turn down the directorship position—life was too short to endure such stress—but I would also quit my thirteen-year job to fulfill a life-long dream to do extended sailing.

My friend Wayne agreed to rent my house while I was gone. His willingness to help me realize my dream seemed like divine intervention.

In December 1991, before setting sail, I visited Vision Mountain one last time. My goal was to take a picture of the place of thunder, where I first heard the song of the universe and where I had encountered "machete man." When I knelt to take a picture something snapped in my camera. Investigating, I found the light meter was broken. Because I had to guess at the light exposure, my overexposed pictures looked washed out when they were developed. Perhaps it was a coincidence, but it seemed to me that the universe did not want me to have a picture of Vision Mountain.

Death weighed heavily on my mind in 1991. My father, a female friend and my beloved ten-year-old cat all died within months of each other. The man who chased me with a machete made me think about the fragility of my life. The deaths and the stress from being acting director at work made life feel hard and short. My supervisor, a two hundred fifty-pound woman with shifty eyes and tight lips, treated me and my co-workers as shirkers to be admonished. A sailing friend from Israel burned the belongings of his mother, who had Alzheimer's disease, when he put her in a nursing home. These events in tandem made me wonder why we work so hard for more possessions that will one day be discarded.

My step-mother, Dorothy, called in May 1991 to let me know my father had died after a two-year battle with cancer. Wanting to attend the funeral in New Orleans, I asked if I could stay with her. "I'm sorry, hon, the house is full," she said curtly.

"May I pitch a tent in your yard?" I asked innocently. "I don't like motels."

"We'll find a bed," she sighed. "But you'll have to make your own way from the airport." Since Dorothy had previously been such a gracious host, her response surprised me, but I agreed to find my own transportation.

For assistance I called Mike, an old friend in New Orleans with whom I sporadically stayed in touch. He was a lawyer and lived with his girlfriend. Mike was sorry to hear about my father and readily agreed to help out. He met me at the airport.

"Does your father have a will?" Mike asked when I mentioned Dorothy's behavior.

"I'm sure he left his estate to Dorothy," I said making myself comfortable in the car.

Mike explained that Louisiana law required that a third of a parent's estate go to the children until the legislation changed the law in January of that year. "I'll find out about the will if you get the name of Dorothy's lawyer," Mike said, glancing at me while he drove. "There's no charge." He clarified further, "Even if your father wrote his will recently, it may be unconstitutional. Although the legislators approved the change, a court case is necessary to find if it's constitutional."

Four relatives besides myself stayed in Dorothy's house. Dorothy and I shared the third bedroom. The funeral went smoothly. When I got back to Macon, I called Dorothy to thank her for her hospitality and asked the name of her lawyer.

Mike sent me a copy of the will a couple months later. It read: "I have a daughter by a previous marriage named Niki LaRocca Collins. I do not leave her any portion of my estate. If the law governing forced heirship should be held unconstitutional, I limit my deed to the lifetime usufruct I give to my wife." (I would inherit after Dorothy's death.) "If my wife predeceases me, I give my entire estate to ..." he named two nephews since I was his only child. My heart raced, and tears came to my eyes. My father had disinherited me two months before he died. He had abandoned me as an infant and rejected me again before his death. Not understanding his motives, I felt hurt. Mike offered to contest the will. I'd pay only the hundred-dollar court fee. The angry child in me was tempted. My father had not paid child support and had avoided seeing me until I contacted him when I was twenty-one. Although we had a rocky relationship, we had kept in touch and I thought he cared for me. I felt betrayed.

After much soul searching, I decided not to contest the will. It did not seem worth the months of litigation, the trauma, and the cost to Dorothy. If his estate were not freely given, I did not want it.

Turning my energy into setting sail on mother ocean would ease my pain, I thought. But it also meant giving up security—thirteen years of experience as a counselor at a Mental Health Center, a steady income, health insurance, retirement, a home and friends. Letting go would not be easy. It felt like jumping off a cliff into the unknown. I drew strength from the previous risks I had taken—starting a new life in America and traveling around the world with Pan Am Airways.

Mike sent me a letter in the fall of 1993. The Louisiana Supreme court had declared the law regarding the abolishment of forced heirship for children in Louisiana to be unconstitutional; I was a forced heir. The news was a relief. I MATTERED! My father finally had to acknowledge me; it was the law.

CHAPTER 11

SETTING SAIL

And the noise of the sea, the eternal roar which mutes and deadens the sense of time, is white noise, containing the rhythms of the planetary system and the drumming of catfish, the whistle of dolphins, the keening of whales.

Elizabeth Borgese

The idea of taking an extended sailing trip took hold the summer of 1991. Each month I scanned the crew-wanted ads of *Cruising World* magazine, but the few leads turned out to be dead ends. Finally, it occurred to me I could write my own ad. Since I had little experience working a boat, I titled my ad "enthusiastic," followed with "attractive, professional female, forty-one, seeks offshore cruising experience." Including my phone number, I volunteered to share expenses.

Satisfied, I thought I would get five or six calls. Instead, for the next three months I found myself sifting through over seventy fabulous offers to sail all over the world.

For a while there was a frenzy of letters, phone calls and visits before I chose Eddie Hausman, a forty-six-year-old marine mechanic from Oregon. He was looking for a crew member not a romance and his black and white Mason 44 named *Luna-Sea* conjured up images of mystery. Focusing on Eddie's offer to visit exotic places on a magnificent boat, I ignored the feeling that I might later question my sanity.

We planned to sail to the Bahamas, the Caribbean islands, Central and South America, the Pacific islands and perhaps around the world. Eddie's life seemed colorful too. He was a bachelor and had earned a living on fishing boats in Alaska.

I looked at my own life: thirteen years working as a children's counselor for a county agency. Although I loved counseling, I missed the wilderness and found the drudgery and sameness of routine stifling. Monday through Friday from eight to five, I felt owned. My work building had no windows, only fluorescent lights. Then there was my personal life—two marriages, two divorces and no children. Also, I had just buried my feline companion of ten years in a tiny grave next to my house. With him went a piece of my heart.

Eddie invited me to sail with him in the Florida Keys over Christmas. It sounded like a perfect opportunity to see if we were compatible. He was candid: "I've had the boat a couple of years, but I've only sailed it about six months."

During lunch at Pumpkin Cay he elaborated. "Drinking was killing me—blackouts—loneliness—depression," he murmured biting into a sandwich. When I hit rock bottom two years ago, I became suicidal and saw a psychiatrist."

"Did you go to AA?

"No, didn't need it. My psychiatrist put me on Lithium and Prozac."

I'd heard of few alcoholics who had "recovered" without AA, but Eddie seemed to be doing well.

"Time to work on the old engine," he said pressing his lips together and disappearing into the engine room.

Eddie looked like a teddy bear with his stocky build, oversized clothes, bald head and red mustache. He enjoyed sailing, but his real love seemed to be tinkering with the engine.

Preparing to do extended sailing was an ordeal. I had to select clothes for cool and warm weather and then get a passport, health insurance, snorkel gear, wet suit, a debit card for my checking account and a first-aid kit. Never having encountered rough seas, I did not know if I were prone to sea sickness.

A friend, who agreed to keep my car, drove me to the boat at Los Olas Boulevard, Fort Lauderdale on January 14, 1992. *Luna-Sea's* tall mast and deck, covered with engine parts, stood out among the motor boats. Since I was used to

Eddie's engine work, I tidied the main cabin, took a food inventory and made dinner. Eddie slept in the main cabin, so I stowed my gear in the bow's V-berth, my new bedroom. For the next three days we bought and stored groceries, filled the boat tanks with fuel and water and ran errands.

Since there was little wind when we left Fort Lauderdale on January 7 it took all day to motor-sail to Key Biscayne. Taking turns at the wheel, we squinted at the water that caught the sunlight in a mass of dazzling silver brilliance. We arrived around sunset and anchored outside Key Biscayne's No-Name Harbor to wait for good weather. A flock of large white egrets with yellow curved bills were roosting in the trees. I gasped with delight.

After eighteen days, Eddie and I were still at Key Biscayne. The egrets' daily return from fishing was my reminder that one day was passing into the next. Arriving one by one, their wings making a slow rowing action through the air, they gave a low, heavy croak before settling on their tall leafy perches.

To get to Bimini, in the Bahamas, we needed to sail fifty miles east of Miami across the hundred-mile-wide and mile-deep north-flowing Gulf Stream. The Gulf Stream carries over thirty million cubic meters of water per second past Miami, more than five times the flow of all the fresh water rivers of the world. Since the prevailing winds came from the east, we were waiting for southerly winds, which usually followed after a cold front. We were told it was unwise to leave during a cold front, for high waves and rough seas occur when the strong northerly winds hit the warm Gulf Stream.

A soft, cool sprinkle of rain tickled my face as I sat on deck in the dark. The wind of the squall was strong and gusting and whistled through the riggings. When the rain became cold and stinging, I turned in. The water hit the hull with a rhythmic splish, splash making the boat bob like a cork.

On Saturday morning, the ocean threw the light back in a fierce flashing glare. A cold front had passed through, and the weather forecast was southeast winds between twenty to twenty-five knots. "Bingo!" Eddie cried, "The wind is what we've been waiting for." Red-faced, he raced across *Luna-Sea*'s deck gathering sail covers. "Niki, stow everything in the cabin!"

While pulling up the anchor we noticed that the twenty-five-knot wind still came from the northeast. I felt apprehensive. "Do you think it's wise to go?" I asked with a shiver. The ocean was foaming in frothy fury, and the white caps were everywhere.

"Yeah; the wind will swing around and settle," Eddie bellowed, lifting the anchor to the deck with a thump. "The waves will flatten in the Gulf Stream, where it's deeper. You'll see."

When we headed for the channel the wind did swing around to the southeast, I noted with relief. But to compensate for the Gulf Stream's northerly current, we had to head the boat south into the breakers. Steep ten-foot angry breaking waves began overwashing the bow. I trembled in fright. "The boat's not making headway!" I gasped from the helm. My knuckles were white from strain.

"If we get to the Gulf Stream, the waves will flatten," Eddie roared from the foredeck. We swung to and fro when ominous waves stormed the vessel.

"Keep her pointed into the wind," Eddie hollered preparing to raise the mainsail. The boat reared like a wild mare in the surge.

"I'm trying," I cried, gripping the wheel tighter. Eddie started to clip the halyard to the sail but the boat lurched upward in a gigantic wave. Whirling like a whip, the halyard flew out of his hand and coiled around the mast.

"Oh shit!" Eddie hissed, jumping back reflexively. He gaped pop-eyed. Terrified, I held my breath. The boat slammed into a trough in the boiling water. His face grew ashen. To retrieve the halyard he unclipped his safety harness from the mast and staggered across the deck to grab a hooked extension pole. Horrified, my skin turned to gooseflesh. Without a safety harness he could fall overboard.

Lumbering back with the pole, he stood on his toes and jumped, but the halyard was too high to reach. The boat rolled again and a wave of foam broke over the bow and splashed into the cockpit with an angry howl. Eddie fell and grabbed at a shroud but was flung against the mast. He clung to the mast to catch his breath. I watched with numbed horror. Regaining his footing, he jumped again and retrieved the halyard. We let out a simultaneous sigh of relief.

"Okay. Bad omens. Let's head back," Eddie murmured clipping his safety harness and the halyard back to the mast. "I'm exhausted!" He was trembling and looked like a ghost. With the wind behind us, we sped back to No-Name Harbor surfing the waves.

At dinner Eddie held up a large stuffed golden bear. "Hi Niki; I'm Quincy," he declared in a deep masculine voice. Surprised, I nodded my head. Clutching a smaller bear, he uttered, "I'm Zack!" in a high-pitched childlike tone. Amused, I responded like-wise. Eddie seemed to relax and become more playful when he spoke through his bears.

I sat alone in the dark on the boat's bow and gazed up at the heavens. The stars made luminous streaks across the sky. I felt grateful to be alive.

January 25 was a cloudless, crisp morning with twenty-knot northeast winds. The waves were five feet, half the size of the previous day. Since the sun's red orb was just above the horizon and the weather seemed favorable, we again prepared to cross the Gulf Stream.

With sails spread and sheets taut, we sailed close into the howling northeast wind. The gray ocean was dotted with white foam and spray. Gigantic waves hissed when they broke over the bow, tumbled across the deck and overwashed the cockpit. Sitting upon the wind, *Luna-Sea* seem to fly across the water, while the ocean, flecked with dancing sunlight, shone like fields of silver. Kept warm and dry by my raingear, I trembled with delight.

"We should see landfall before dark," Eddie said, peering over my shoulder at the oceans, warm golden tone in the dimming light.

"Yup, there it is!" he said proudly, pointing to a faint gray line on the northeastern horizon. "Take the wheel," he whooped, leaping down the companionway. "I need to recheck the GPS bearings."

A couple of minutes later he emerged smiling. "We're a little south of my reckoning; let's ease the boat upwind," he declared taking the wheel and turning her to port. When the world receded into darkness, we took down the sails and motored, squinting into the night.

"Eddie, I can see trees!" I cried, trembling.

"It'll be another thirty minutes before landfall." Eddie reassured me.

"Are you sure?" I responded wide-eyed. The tall dark silhouettes looked like trees.

"Boom, crack!" *Luna-Sea*'s fiberglass hull hit coral. We shot forward and fell against the wheel. The boat shuddered and stopped. "Oh, shit!" Eddie spat. "We've hit the island!" I gaped in stunned silence.

"Crunch! Crunch!" The boat's bow pounded against the coral each time a wave hit. Dazed and shivering, I flew like a shot into the forward cabin. "No leaks," I yelled with relief.

To start up the engine, Eddie jerked the gear into reverse. "Shit! The gear is jammed in neutral," he bellowed. "The engine is useless." He grabbed his Danforth anchor and threw it behind the boat, then tried without success to winch us off the coral with the anchor line.

The "hum" of a boat engine broke the din on deck. Two white lights appeared. "Maybe we can get help," I said hopefully.

"I don't need them," Eddie mumbled through clenched teeth. "I hope they stay away!" The boat receded into the darkness. Astonished, I remained silent.

Finally, after forty-five minutes of frantic struggling with the engine and anchors, *Luna-Sea* drifted free. The tide had turned. Eddie pulled up the stern anchor, allowed the boat to drift into deeper water, then threw out the bow anchor. We prepared for the night. The boat rolled from side to side in the ocean swell and clattered. It was two hours past midnight.

The next morning we discovered we had run aground on the northeast side of Gun Cay, an island in the Bimini chain. According to the *Cruising Guide to the Bahamas* Gun Cay is ten miles south of Alice Town, the largest settlement on North Bimini Island. Ernest Hemingway brought fame to the area in the late 1920s, and many of his memorabilia are on display at the Complete Angler Bar in Alice Town.

The Bimini Islands are part of the seven-hundred Bahamian islands and over two-thousand cays (pronounced "keys") covering one hundred thousand square miles. They are the exposed tips of two large submarine plateaux, the Great and Little Bahama Banks, which are from sixteen to sixty-five feet deep. The Great Bahama bank is split by a deep chasm called the Tongue of the Ocean on one side and by the Exuma Sound on the other. The banks are made of almost pure calcium carbonate and are one of the few places where lime is still being deposited.

"I don't know how we got off course," Eddie said wistfully. "It was a bad mistake! If you want to go back to the States, I'll take you," he said pressing his lips together and looking at the floor.

"It's okay," I said firmly. "But sometimes I fear for our safety."

Eddie's blue eyes filled with tears. "Thanks; I feel I don't deserve companionship at times," he whispered and blinked furiously, but the tears remained. "I'll be more careful!"

Eddie's lips stayed pressed together as he fixed the boat's gears. Twenty-six hours later the gears were operating sufficiently well to motor a mile south to North Cat Cay to clear customs. It was January 28. North Cat Cay was quiet and clean with amiable people. There were no cars, only golf carts, and the chickens ran free.

Having sailed in the Bimini Islands before, I had fond memories. Friendly fish had escorted us while we snorkeled, entranced, above a path of huge stone formations off North Bimini Island. Many people believe the twenty feet deep stones belong to the lost continent of Atlantis.

Most scholars put the arrival of the Lucayan Indians in the Bahamas at around 900 A.D. They called their country Bajamar, "islands of the shallow sea." Fifty years after Columbus' landing in 1492, practically the entire Lucayan race had been destroyed. In 1629 the English formally claimed the Bahamas from its Indian and Spanish Inhabitants. But it was in 1783 that the Bahamas were permanently ceded to the British, ending three hundred years of disputed ownership.

During the years of the Prohibition, between 1920 and 1933, the Bahamas enjoyed an era of prosperity. Nassau, Grand Bahama Island and Bimini became busy ports for both American and Bahamian rum runners. With the repeal of Prohibition in 1933 and the worldwide Great Depression, the Bahamian economy suffered until tourism took hold in the 1950s. In 1964 the Bahamas was granted internal self government and in 1969 the islands became known as the Commonwealth of the Bahamas with a ministerial form of government.

Eighty-five percent of the Bahamian citizens are of African origin and twelve percent are of European or mixed descent. Most Bahamians speak English in a rhythmic dialect with lilts and nuances akin to dialects in the other Caribbean islands. Tourism accounts for about seventy percent of the Bahamas' gross national product.

We motored back to Gun Cay, and anchored on the eastern side of the island. A thin veil of clouds crept across the sky. That night the southeast wind began to howl. Large ocean swells rocked the boat, and everything not secured fell or rattled, keeping us awake.

The next day I was tired, and my patience with Eddie was short. He seemed to feel the same way, for we snapped at each other. When Eddie said, "Salt is hard on boats; we've got to get rid of it," for the fifth time I snapped. "Eddie, you're obsessed with salt water. You should consider fresh water sailing."

Eddie turned white. "I feel betrayed and victimized," he roared. He reached for his tools and opened the engine room door. "You seemed so kind, a pleasant personality," he sneered.

"A pleasant personality," I repeated raising my voice. "So I can't get angry?" I fumed. Eddie pressed his lips together, grabbed a wrench and plunged into the engine room.

To cool off, I snorkeled to Gun Cay and hiked across the beach. The sun felt warm and nurturing. Pieces of driftwood, seaweed, shells, tangles of roots and human trash marked the high-water line. Brilliantly-pigmented fiddler crabs scurried across the hot sand on their toes, occasionally stopping to eat a microscopic plant or animal.

Becoming darker by day and lighter by night fiddler crabs blend with the beach. Their burrows and chambers with slanting tunnels just above the mid-tide line never flood because they line their homes with wet sand and plug the entrance. To repair the burrow they roll up balls of sand and carry them to the surface.

After a long swim I lay on the warm sand and listened to the rhythmic swirling waves pounding the shore. Closing my eyes, I reflected that I had been pleasant, but that the frustration of the past two weeks had surfaced, finding an easy target in Eddie. I decided to apologize.

The ocean sparkled in the sunlight when I hiked back along a ridge. Coconut palm trees grew along the narrow strip just above the high-water mark, their large, brown, edible, hard-shelled seeds, the coconuts, hung in clusters. I'm told that coconuts can stay alive at sea for as long as four months. When I got to the boat I found Eddie in the engine room and apologized. He nodded but did not look up.

At sunrise we started a seventy-mile sail southeast to Chub Cay, the first of twenty-six islands in the Berry Islands. Careening clouds flapped and raced across the sky. We sailed close-hauled into light northeasterly winds with ten other boats. Sailing ahead of the group, we anchored near Russell Light. When the other boats did not appear at sunset we were mystified. Through the binoculars we spied a circle of boats anchored at a distance. Eddie checked his bearings and found we were two miles off course. The next morning we corrected our course and caught up with the boats.

The wind began to freshen and the seas became choppy with breaking waves. "Bloody wind!" Eddie snorted. The other boats dropped their mainsails and used their jibs. Eddie put a reef in both sails. "Let's get ahead," Eddie yelled when we passed the boats. *Luna-Sea* began to heel wildly.

"Take the helm, Niki. We have too much sail!" Eddie shouted staggering toward the bow. "I'll put another reef in the sails."

My eyes blinked from the spray as I tried to keep her headed into the wind. The boom accidentally whipped across the boat with a loud crack. My pulse quickened. If the boom swung again, it could hit Eddie on the head and throw him overboard. I trembled with fear. "Let's just use the jib," I pleaded.

It took three attempts to get the sail in and we were exhausted. Then, when we arrived at Chub Cay we were disappointed to find there were no good anchorages out of the wind and swell. We continued on to Little Whale Cay. Two other boats were anchored to the right of a cut near the beach. Because our experience navigating through the coral heads was minimal, we anchored farther out.

Eddie studied the engine room and announced. "I'm going to work on the engine tomorrow." He pressed his lips together. "The exhaust pipe connection is loose and the room is filling with smoke." Feeling tired and bewildered, I said nothing. It had become difficult to live around Eddie, but I squelched the temptation to give up. I was determined to complete my adventure.

At daybreak a cold wind continued to blow out of the northeast making it too cold to swim or snorkel. While Eddie worked on the engine, I read and reminisced about a previous sailing trip in the area. When the *Bahama Star*, our sailboat, had left the cut at Little Whale Cay, we lamented that we had never swum with porpoises. As if on command, the prominent gray dorsal fins of two adults and a baby bottle-nosed dolphin had leaped and dove through the air when they cut across the water to the boat. Grabbing our snorkels we had jumped in the water. With tails moving in an undulating motion they had swirled around us, gazing into our eyes and smiling with their open beak-like, toothy jaws. We had been saddened when they left.

I remembered with awe how dolphins were once a land animal and have a sophisticated communication system we don't understand with up to thirty whistle and click sounds.

While we were having dinner the wind picked up and began to howl. Eddie finished his meal. "We're leaving for Nassau tomorrow," he said giving me a sidelong glance.

"Can't we see more of the Berrys?" I asked wistfully.

"No, we need to go. I want to be in the Dominican Republic by March," Eddie said firmly.

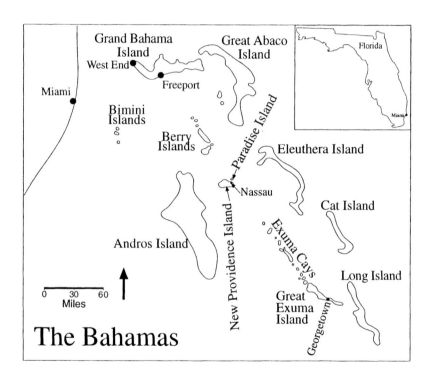

The Bahamas

CHAPTER 12

LUNA-SEA

Every woman's womb is a micro-ocean, the salinity of its fluid resembling that of primeval waters; and every micro-ocean restages the drama of the origin of life in the gestation of every embryo, from one cell protozoan through all the phases of gill-breathing and amphibian, to mammalian evolution. And every human, in turn, is a planet ocean, for 71 percent of his substance consists of salty water, just as 71 percent of the earth is covered by the oceans. ...The last act of the drama of the oceans is on the stage. We must save our oceans if we are to save ourselves.

Elizabeth Borgese

We sailed to Nassau on a beam reach (at a ninety-degree angle to the wind) on February 2. The boat rolled in the six-foot ocean swell. When we arrived at Nassau Harbor later in the afternoon, four huge cruise ships, speeding motor boats and noisy shore action broke the ocean's gentle lapping sound.

Nassau Harbor is the bay between Paradise and New Providence Islands and has strong currents. To prevent the boat anchor from dragging when the tide turns, boats are required to set two anchors, one off the bow and one off the stern. Neither Eddie nor I was accustomed to this practice. Eddie requested I steer while he threw out the anchors. Then he motored to the anchors to see if they would hold. They usually didn't.

After a couple of hours, we were tired and irritable from trying to set the two anchors. Another boat owner came over. "If your boat drifts, it'll hit mine," the captain drawled.

"I'm doing the best I can," Eddie said, turning white. Two hours later Eddie was satisfied with the anchors.

When we awoke the next morning the boat was rolling. Our anchorage opposite the Yoga Retreat was not protected from the swells of an easterly wind. To our surprise the anchors held. Our anchorage opposite Swami Vishnu

Divanananda's Yoga retreat brought back fond memories, for I had stayed there to learn yoga for eight days in 1981.

Wisps of drifting clouds came by after breakfast. We took the inflatable dinghy to the Basra dock on the Nassau shoreline. While Eddie ordered engine parts I explored Nassau. Three cruise ships dominated the skyline like giant steel mountains. Passengers from the boats scurried around Bay Street and the straw market and terns wheeled on the wind in graceful arabesques.

An arched toll bridge connects the twenty-one mile long New Providence Island to the four-mile long Paradise Island. Paradise Island was known as Hog Island before Hunting Hartford changed its name in 1960. The world became aware of Nassau in the early 1940s when the Duke and Duchess of Windsor became the First Family of the islands.

Eddie and I planned to meet at the dock at four to return to the boat, but at five he had not yet arrived. A dark-haired man with graying temples kept pacing and looking around as if he were also waiting. He introduced himself as Gaylin from the boat *Morning Star* and asked if I needed a ride. We began to talk.

When Eddie strolled over, Gaylin expressed an interest in Eddie's engine problem since he had fixed something similar a few years ago. "Come and look at my set up this evening, Eddie," Gaylin offered when we left. Eddie visited with Gaylin after dinner and was impressed.

"I'm going to rebuild a part of my engine and will need to order some parts," Eddie announced. "It'll probably be a few weeks before we'll leave Nassau." Since Nassau was a large noisy city, I was disappointed.

On Tuesday morning we decided to move *Luna-Sea* closer to Nassau City on the south side of the harbor. We pulled up the anchor near the Yoga Retreat at sunrise, but five hours later we were still motoring the boat backwards and forwards. A number of boat occupants looked on with amused expressions while relaxing on their decks.

Embarrassed, I wished the earth would open up and swallow me.

"Can we take a break?" I inquired around noon. Eddie nodded, beads of sweat dotted his forehead.

"Shouldn't we ask someone about anchoring?" I suggested when I returned. Eddie's face paled.

"I knew I was in for an earful!" A thin film of perspiration formed on his upper lip, "How dare you suggest I don't know what I am doing." He tightened his lips and searched among his tools. "I expect you to be supportive, not turn against me."

"I'm sorry," I pleaded, my stomach in knots.

"You don't have to help. I'll do it myself," he muttered through clenched teeth. He disappeared below deck. A few minutes later he reappeared in a bathing suit, snorkel and mask, dove overboard, and physically adjusted the anchors. Stunned, I collapsed on deck and thought how the other boat owners seem to throw out their anchors and drift backwards till their boats held. They did not motor to the anchor, like Eddie. All attempts to apologize were met with silence.

"Eddie, should I find another boat?" I asked while we were eating dinner.

Eddie chewed his food thoughtfully. "I think it's best!" he agreed.

The food became tasteless. "I guess you're right," I shivered, my brain awhirl. "May I stay on your boat till I find another?"

"That's fine," Eddie said curtly looking at his feet. He looked up. "I reread the chapter on anchoring. I have a lot to learn; it was embarrassing to have people watch."

For the next two days Eddie and I remained cordial, but I noticed he put away his stuffed bears. With a heavy heart I posted signs at two marinas and told the other yacht occupants I was available to crew.

Making meals and washing up continued to be my chore. During the day I sought refuge on the beach at Paradise

Island. Eddie took me to the Basra dock and fetched me from there unless I hitched a ride with someone else. To get to Paradise Island I walked down Nassau harbor, crossed the arched bridge and followed a path through the woods to the beach.

Some days I sat on a bluff overlooking the ocean. Listening to the hypnotic rhythm of the surf pounding the rocks and watching the water catch the sunlight in blinding brilliance, I found peace. When I invited Eddie to join me, he declined, saying he had work to do.

One day a young man with a snorkel and mask emerged from the sea and smiled at me. "What's the snorkeling like?" I asked.

"It's okay. I've seen better," he said sitting down next to me. The story of my struggle with Eddie tumbled out.

"I'm impressed with what you're doing," he said admiringly. "It takes a lot of courage." The man and his wife were on vacation in Fort Lauderdale and had taken a one-day flight to Paradise Island. He laughed when he heard my boat's name. "*Luna-Sea*; that figures!" Although we spoke only a short time, I felt better.

When I arrived at the dock, *Luna-Sea*'s dinghy was tied up and locked. Because of the high incidence of theft, locking the engine was a common safety practice. A dense column of rain blotted out the world. During my hour-long wait I took cover under the Basra house porch.

When Eddie and I reached the boat, I had a headache and felt nauseated. "Eddie, I can't face making food tonight," I groaned from my bunk.

With hands in his pockets and lips pressed tight, Eddie paced the cabin. He stuck his head in my berth, "Would you like Zack and Quincy?" he asked softly. "I need to work on the engine."

"Thanks," I moaned.

"They're glad you're here," he muttered putting the stuffed bears next to me. Then he left.

At sunrise dark clouds drained the world of light, but I felt better. According to the VHF radio there would be rain squalls and gale warnings the next two days. One sailboat drifted downstream and became grounded near the Yoga Retreat. *Luna-Sea* swung too far to the northwest and came within a couple of feet of a catamaran. We watched nervously. Instead of going to Paradise Island, I baked bread and read. Eddie and I were tense.

When the wind swept across the water between rain squalls, the waves lapped around the boat's hull with a rhythmic, "splish, splash." Despite the heavy rains, the cabin was warm and dry. I loved hearing the water sloshing against the cabin's womb-like belly. The throbbing sounded like a mother's heart-beat.

Bill, a stern-looking skipper of the boat *Rising Star*, invited me to crew with him starting February 13. Concerned about compatibility, I decided not to go. Eddie said I could stay on *Luna-Sea*, but I was determined to find another boat. Since it was a dull, rainy day, I baked muffins.

"Niki, would you mind winching me up the mast?" Eddie asked while eating a muffin. I looked up at the mast.

"I've never done that before. Is it safe?" I asked nervously.

"There's nothing to it!" Eddie said briskly. He sat in the bosun's chair, which is designed for going up the mast, and clipped himself to the main halyard.

To my amazement, I winched him up the mast with little effort. Eddie finished his work and asked to come down. My heart beat faster. "Oh, no!" I yelled. "I can't release you. The halyard is tangled in the winch." My mouth went dry.

Eddie looked around and blinked. "That's okay. I'll stand on the spreaders to take the weight off the halyard," he said reassuringly from up the mast. Disentangling the snarl, I lowered Eddie without further problems.

There was a continuous racket of bulldozers and drills at a building site on the Nassau shoreline. The "clang, clang" of halyards and sheets hitting the sailboat masts, and the waves lapping against the side of the boat punctuated the din. When the noise from the electronic equipment made me feel tense, I sought refuge in Eddie's books. My first was J.E. Lovelock's *Gaia* about the earth's being a single living entity, not a demented spaceship forever traveling driverless and purposeless around an inner circle of the sun. It reminded me of the Native American's view of the earth being interconnected and sacred. Another inspiring book was Riane Eisler's *The Chalice and the Blade*. She outlined the feminine and the Goddess as a force in history and spoke of collaborative societies in the past in which neither sex dominated. She gave me hope for the future. Joseph Campbell's *Hero with a Thousand Faces* made our sailing adventure seem like a hero's journey. We too had left the security of city life for an adventure on Mother Ocean and would, hopefully, return with new knowledge and wisdom.

The following day I explored the eastern shoreline of Paradise Island. I walked under the blazing sun past hotels and condos to a deserted beach. A small hawksbill turtle surfaced for air while I lazed under a palm tree in the sun. The turtle's brown shield-like shell and long broad flippers were motionless as it floated with its beak-like head in the air.

I'm told these intelligent reptile air breathers have lungs but also get oxygen from the water via gill-like cloaca, enabling them to stay under water for long periods. For centuries people have taken the shells of the hawksbill turtle by burning or boiling the shell off, then returning the poor creature to the ocean thinking it will survive. Although turtles can live up to a hundred fifty years, their numbers have decreased and they are suffering, some catastrophically, from our economic predation and the destruction of their habitat.

The turtle dove and disappeared when a big open boat called *Yellow Bird* sailed up. Calypso music and chatter replaced the gentle sound of the ocean lapping at the shoreline. When two hundred passengers disembarked, I wandered away, back down the beach.

At dawn I was awakened by a plink, plink sound. Two twigs had fallen through the hatch above my bed. Astonished, I sat up to look through the opening. A small brown bird was building a nest on the top of our swaying mast. The bird had been hard at work, as evidenced by the branches covering the deck. Stirred by the bird's industry, I wondered how many times I, like the bird, had persevered under impossible conditions.

Three sailboats left at daybreak, leaving fourteen boats in our anchorage. I longed to leave also and thought seriously about flying home. The chilly breeze from the northeast made the air cold.

Living on another person's boat and not knowing the future had become frightening. Instead of making plans to leave, I occupied myself doing laundry and treated myself to a hot fresh-water shower at a yacht club down the street. Usually we used sea water to bathe and rinsed off with warm fresh water from a sun shower on deck. The black lower lining of the plastic sunshower bag absorbs the sun's heat through the clear upper wall and the water in the bag becomes hot.

I checked at the Yacht clubs but there were no inquiries about my ad to crew. I felt even more despondent. When I arrived at the Basra dock at noon Eddie was in the dinghy. His lips were pressed tight. "The boat is dragging anchor," he muttered. He spent the afternoon diving in the water to move the anchors to various positions. "I'm not sure the anchors are going to hold," Eddie moaned at dinner. "But I'm calling it a day."

On Sunday morning Gaylin stopped at our boat on his way to the dock to invite us to dinner on Monday night. He and his wife had returned from Eleuthera the previous night. Starved for company, I accepted and looked forward to the visit. Twelve days had passed since I started looking for a boat. With only one offer, I felt discouraged and wondered if I should have sailed with *Rising Star*.

While lazing on the beach at Paradise Island on Monday morning, I noticed two men and a woman shampooing their hair. Guessing they were from a boat, I approached the tanned-looking younger man. "Are you from a sailboat?" I asked, my pulse quickening.

"Yes. I'm with Cal and Sandy from the boat, *Hopscotch*," he said with a smile and gestured towards an older couple. His name was Jason. We discovered, to our delight, that our boats were anchored near each other. Sandy and Cal joined us. Cal, the owner of *Hopscotch*, was a retired police officer from New York. Sandy, a slender blonde, had been sailing in Costa Rica before she hooked up with Cal, but this was Jason's first sailing trip. They planned to sail with Cal through May before going back to other jobs. Cal and his crew gave me a ride back to *Luna-Sea* in his dinghy.

At dinner I told Gaylin and Julie, his wife, I was looking for another boat. They laughed when they heard I was lonely because Eddie worked all the time. Gaylin looked thoughtful. "I met an interesting young man this morning," he said scratching his head. "He has two sea kayaks on his sailboat."

"I love sea kayaking," I said, trying not to tremble with excitement.

"Really!" Gaylin responded with a laugh. "I think his name is Joe. There's an article in *Sea Kayak*er magazine about his solo kayaking from Grenada to Puerto Rico. "He looked up and smiled. "He's your man!"

"What's his boat's name?" I asked eagerly. Gaylin thought a moment.

"I can't remember. Look for the smallest sailboat." A rush of energy made me feel I would sail with Joe. Gaylin seemed like a guardian angel.

At first light I looked for the smallest sailboat among the fifty boats anchored in the area. To spot the more distant boats I got out the binoculars. A little sailboat with a white sea kayak lashed to her lifelines and rigging came into view. Her name was *Y-Not*. My heart beat faster. A tall, bearded sandy-haired man in his thirties started up the outboard engine, pulled up the anchor, and left. I was crushed.

When I awoke Tuesday morning I realized that *Y-Not* had returned during the night and was anchored a short distance from our boat. I felt a rush of excitement. My heart was pounding when I rowed over to *Y-Not*'s empty deck.

"Hi, hello!" I yelled. A bare-foot tanned, muscular man in a blue bathing suit stepped out into the companionway.

"Hi, I'm Niki," I said, waving.

"I'm Joe Waters. Come aboard." A big bronze hand helped me onto the deck and I plopped down on the cockpit seat.

"Gaylin said you're a sea kayaker. I sea-kayaked in Costa Rica a couple of years ago and loved it!"

"Oh, really!" he responded, his clear blue eyes held mine with a steady gaze. "Would you like something to drink: coffee, tea, juice?"

"Tea sounds good, thanks," I said making myself comfortable and mopping my brow. Joe lit the alcohol stove within view. He reminded me of a lion with his imposing countenance; proud, erect body; bushy beard and brown wind-swept mane of hair. His large six-foot frame dwarfed the boat making it look like a toy.

"I'm from Florida, New York. I'm writing a book about sea kayaking in the Bahamas," Joe volunteered with an air of calm assurance.

"I'm impressed. Gaylin said you solo kayaked from Grenada to Puerto Rico."

"Oh, yeah. It was quite an adventure!" He gave a deep infectious belly laugh.

Embarrassed about my trip's purpose, I blurted, "I'm looking for a boat to sail to Georgetown."

"You can sail with me," he responded in a slow considered way. "If you don't mind a small boat."

"I'd love to!" I said, relieved.

However, there were problems: Joe was expecting two sea kayaking friends in a couple of days; his sister and her husband for a week starting April 3, and he was flying to the States to work for awhile shortly thereafter.

"My friends and I will be sailing and sea kayaking in the north Exumas for six days," he said thoughtfully. "But we'll be back on February 28. You can move aboard then." I was ecstatic.

When I returned to *Luna-Sea*, Eddie was in the engine room. "I found a boat," I said excitedly. "It's the sea kayaker Gaylin recommended!"

"The sea kayaker, eh!" Eddie mumbled. He glanced up, then continued working on the engine with renewed vigor.

Since Joe had two free days before his friends arrived, he had offered to take me sea kayaking in his Klepper.

The following morning, we paddled five miles east of Nassau to Cable Beach for a picnic. Dark shadows of low cumulus clouds ran across the water.

"I used this boat on my Caribbean trip," Joe said wistfully. I was amazed to learn that Kleppers were so sturdy they've crossed the Atlantic and gone around Cape Horn.

On a small island's shifting spit of sand opposite Cable Beach we ate the tuna sandwiches I'd made. "I'm a millwright," Joe said gravely. "The work is dangerous, but the pay is good and it allows me to take off." His eyes held a faraway look, "My girlfriend and I broke up after dating three years. She tried sailing but didn't like it. She went back to New York two weeks ago."

"I'm sorry."

"Yeah thanks. But it's for the best," Joe whispered, eyeing the sand. "I'm not cut out for relationships." Sifting through the sand with his fingers, he muttered, "I'm a loner and marriage phobic." A black and white laughing gull landed on the beach and chuckled, "ha-hah-hah-hah."

Returning to Joe's boat, we started back. "My father was an alcoholic and left my family when I was young," Joe said mournfully. "I saw my father again two years ago, and it was a disappointment. He was cold and distant, and he was still drinking."

"I grew up without a father, too, and was disillusioned when we met," I commiserated. The loneliness from two months of isolation with Eddie melted. It was like leaving the arctic snow for the tropics.

At first light we took a two-hour sail south of Nassau to a small uninhabited beach on Rose Island. Dazzled by the bright sunshine, I thought the sky seemed bluer and the ocean's sparkle more silver.

Reeling from the staggering display of beauty, we snorkeled among giant vibrating red, orange and brown coral gardens. The delicate lace-like multi-colored sea fans waved in unison with the current, capturing food from the water. Brilliantly colored tropical fish swam as if suspended on the ocean's blue stage.

I was fascinated to learn that a coral reef is the oldest ecosystem on earth, beginning over two-billion years ago, and that the coral are really colonies of animals that consist of a jelly-like body enclosed in a skeleton of calcium carbonate with a hollow digestive system and an opening at the top. Because of the ice ages, the Caribbean coral is only five-thousand years old. Isolated from the Indo-Pacific, the Caribbean coral developed distinct differences, and out of a hundred endemic hard corals, only eight are shared.

Marine biologists say the proposal to replace the Panama Canal with a sea level water-way to allow the passage of ships from the Caribbean to the Indo-Pacific would be a catastrophe for marine life. Competition, alien species, new diseases and predators like the crown of thorns starfish, which is threatening the Pacific coral, would also threaten the Caribbean's reefs.

Joe dove among the coral and fish, his brown body looking as graceful as a porpoise. He seemed as much at home in the ocean as he did on land. Hallowed by the fish and the flames of the falling sun, I returned content.

After breakfast, I took a loaf of freshly-baked bread to Joe. He and his friends left about thirty minutes later. It was sad to say goodbye.

A cool salty, breeze wafted down the hatch. Eddie joined me for lunch. "I got the parts for the engine yesterday. They won't take long to install," Eddie said, focusing on the boat's wheel. "I'll be leaving Nassau in three days."

"Joe will be back on the 28," I mused. "I'll find somewhere else to stay for the four days." Eddie looked away. The Yoga Retreat seemed the best option at fifty dollars a day. The prices of other hotels were about the same but did not include meals.

After a swim on Paradise Island, I got a ride back to the boat with Walt, a somber-looking retired professor of communications. He was single-handing a forty-foot boat called *Adele-T*. Since Joe planned to leave his boat in Georgetown and go back to work in April, I talked with Walt about returning to the States on his boat.

Heinz, a boyish looking bearded man from the boat *Traumtanzer*, stopped to visit on February 23. He was from Canada and expected his girlfriend to join him on March 1. When he heard I needed a place to stay, he offered his boat. Relieved, I accepted and marveled how Great Spirit provided what I needed.

The next two days Eddie left the engine room only for meals. A din of muttering came from the engine room. The day before Eddie was due to sail south, strong blustering winds came from the direction he was going. "I'm leaving tomorrow for Rose Island to wait for better weather," Eddie said curtly.

"I'll move to *Traumtanzer*," I said gloomily. Eddie nodded.

Later that afternoon I talked to Jason and Sandy on Paradise Island and my spirits lifted. Sandy said she had sailed as paid crew for a wealthy man on a sixty-foot boat for two months in Costa Rica. "The job was hard. I cleaned, cooked, and helped dock the boat and got yelled at all the time," she said mournfully. "I was glad when the trip ended."

Eddie gave me a few groceries, since we had split the cost. Relieved, I thought my ordeal was over, but greater trials were yet to come.

A fierce wind whined on February 25. Eddie went ashore to finish his errands in Nassau. Cal, Sandy and Jason stopped by to exchange addresses. "Thanks for talking to Sandy about her bad experience," Cal said, cranking up the dinghy's motor. "Joe seems like a good man." It was sad to see them leave.

When Eddie returned, Heinz brought his boat alongside Eddie's to get my gear. "Thanks for everything, Eddie!" I said giving him a hug.

"You're welcome," Eddie said hurriedly, placing my duffel bag on Heinz's boat. He returned to the wheel and shot back in reverse missing a boat by inches. Stopping just in time, he motored forward and took off at full throttle. Watching him leave, I felt strangely disembodied.

After Heinz and I stowed my gear, we had dinner and talked about ourselves. Heinz was a psychologist as was his companion, Marlena. He did research, but she was a therapist, like me. The four days passed quickly with lots of talks, walks and errands.

Cold, gusty winds prevailed on Friday, February 28, the day of Joe's expected arrival from the Exumas. Since he would be sailing into the shrieking winds, his return was questionable. When I went to bed at ten, Joe had still not appeared, and I was disappointed.

Since Heinz was expecting his girlfriend on Sunday, I started to look for another boat after breakfast. On the way to the East Bay Marina, Joe's and my designated place to leave messages, Heinz and I met Maurice, a dark-haired Canadian in his thirties who made a living delivering boats. When he heard I needed a place to stay, he volunteered one of his vacant delivery boats.

To my delight, Joe was already at the East Bay Marina trying to locate me. "We had engine trouble about sixteen miles south of Nassau and had to tack into the wind and heavy seas," Joe explained when we hugged. "We made it to Nassau at nine and anchored a few miles away on the eastern shore."

CHAPTER 13

Y-NOT

But ask the beasts, and they shall teach thee; and the fowls of the air, they shall teach thee.

Job 12:7

One generation passes away, another is born: but the earth lives forever.

Ecclesiastes 1:4

On Saturday morning, I transferred and sorted through my belongings while Joe repaired a crack in his boat's water tank.

"*Y-Not*'s got a hole in her bow," he declared, his face a marvel of solemnity.

"Are we sinking?" I asked astonished. Noticing his amused expression, I relaxed.

"We'll fix it with this!" He chuckled holding up a small silver can.

After breakfast we stopped at the marina to tell Maurice I no longer needed his boat. He turned to Joe, "It's your fault; you should have stayed in the Exuma Islands." We laughed.

The next morning Joe worked on the boat's hole while I did last-minute shopping. We planned to leave Nassau for Green Turtle Cay later that day.

"Niki, take the tiller while I get the anchor," Joe said, strolling to the bow at noon. "She's up!" Joe yelled. The anchor landed on deck.

Being unfamiliar with Joe's outboard engine, I turned the throttle too far. *Y-Not* shot forward towards a large sailboat. "Ahhhh!" I screamed. The two men on deck jumped back, their eyes wide. Joe sprang to my side, grabbed the tiller and turned *Y-Not* away from the boat.

"I'm sorry!" I groaned, trembling with fright.

"That's okay!" Joe responded good-naturedly. "You'll have to excuse her," he yelled to the men. "She's still learning." The two men smiled and waved.

We sailed with a tail wind behind us to Green Turtle Cay, a deserted island about sixteen miles south of Nassau. The sun played peek-a-boo with the clouds, and the wind brought the scent of fresh sea air.

Joe's trolling line went taut. "I think my line's caught on coral," he groaned, "Niki, throw out the anchor. I need to get my snorkel gear." He dove in the direction of the line and surfaced with a grin. "It's a grouper," he yelled. "Hand me my spear; it backed into a hole." Joe grilled the grouper for dinner that evening.

Y-Not's two-and-a-half-foot draft allowed us to anchor close to the shore of Green Cay's white beach surrounded by clear, turquoise water. A sunset graced the horizon and the island's black silhouette seemed aflame in brilliant reds. The air became still. Hypnotized by the rhythm of the water lapping against the bow, we sat spellbound. Ribbons of stars exploded into view and sparkled in the darkness.

Joe slept on a large double bed in the bow. My bed was opposite the galley on a small bunk. With my head facing the open companionway, puffs of cool salty air caressed my face. There was a faint smell of seaweed.

We set sail for Ship's Channel Cay in the Exumas at daybreak. Cutting silently through water turned silver by the morning sun, *Y-Not*'s white sails billowed in the breeze. Heading south, we ran with the wind behind us.

Ships Channel Cay is thirty-five miles southeast of Nassau and is the first of the three hundred and sixty-five Exuma islands, a hundred-mile-long chain.

We anchored with four other sailboats in a clear blue channel of water sandwiched between two hilly islands. After lunch we explored the cliffs on the north end of the island. We paddled tandem in the sea-kayak, with Joe in the stern. Since I was using new muscles, the paddling strokes were hard, but it became easier once I got into a rhythm. When the white jagged bluffs towered above us, we hiked to the cliff's summit. From the top the five sailboats looked like miniature toys floating in the bay, and the clusters of coral appeared as dark patches in the turquoise ocean.

The VHF radio forecast clear skies and gentle breezes for the next couple of days. At sunrise we packed the Klepper with camping gear and food and started a ten-mile trip around Ships Channel Cay. We stopped for lunch on a grassy hill at a small uninhabited island called Signal Cay. The ruins of an old lighthouse stood nearby.

A dark brown osprey with a whitish head and black lines through its eyes sat in a twiggy nest on top of a decaying fence post. It gave an occasional "cheep, cheep." Another osprey flapped slowly above the water, then hovered for a few seconds before half-closing its wings to plunge deep into the sea. It reemerged with a fish in its talons and carried it to the occupied nest. With great "peeps" of excitement, two babies probed down the throat of the adult for the regurgitated predigested fish.

Osprey are the only hawks that dive into the water. Living up to twenty-one years, they were once almost exterminated. I was fascinated to learn that over ninety percent of all birds form pairs and share the parental duties. Sadly, seventy percent of the bird species in the world are in decline.

After lunch we returned to Ships Channel Cay to look for a camp site. The first beach, after a two-hour paddle, was on the island's east side next to a sparkling blue lagoon. We pitched the tent near the lagoon's entrance, hoping it would stay dry at high tide .

Since it was low tide, we explored the lagoon. A small school of silver fish and a bluish-green diamond-shaped trigger fish followed our boat, to our amazement. We were thrilled to see a deer's tiny hoof print dotting the shore when we beached the kayak.

Sitting in the dark outside our tent, Joe told me about his solo kayak trip a few years earlier. "I visited twelve islands in a four-month period. The hundred-and-ten-mile Anegada Passage between St. Martin and Tortola was my longest paddle. The passage lived up to its reputation for being windy and stormy with strong currents," Joe drawled. "Thirty-knot winds blew the tops off ten-to-twelve foot breaking waves. I paddled for twenty-eight hours straight, bracing frequently," he said gravely. "Taking half-hour breaks to sleep, I was afraid if I stopped I would be blown out to the middle of the Caribbean." I was impressed and told him so.

"That wasn't the hardest part," Joe said quietly. "When I left Tortola for Vieques I was hit by a hurricane. The twenty-five-foot waves came from behind and picked up my kayak, making me surf faster than the boat could go. Zigzagging back and forth through the waves, I tried to stay on course. The storm blew my boat twenty miles off course, and I ended up in Culebra." His voice trailed off into the darkness.

It felt good to sleep on Mother Earth, and we both slept soundly. The water had not reached us at high tide, we discovered with relief.

We returned to *Y-Not* for lunch. A Canadian couple, Manuel and Isabella, showed us a forty-pound grouper and three bright red lobsters they had caught on the east side of Ships Channel Cay. "We worried when you did not return. Since your boat was locked, we thought you might be out overnight," Manuel, a short balding man, said thoughtfully.

Joe gathered his spear fishing equipment to try his luck. Even with a wet suit, the cold water ignited my nerve endings. While Joe fished, my eyes followed a brilliant green parrot fish as it bit into chunks of coral to get at the algae. I heard they are able to grind up the coral and excrete it and often start life as a female and later change to a male.

Shoals of small bright-blue damsel fish hovered around the antler coral collecting organic food particles. Coral reefs are known as the jungles of the sea, and the waves that break across the coral saturate the water with oxygen. Reefs exist only where the water temperature is not likely to fall below seventy degrees.

When Joe returned with a small Nassau grouper and two large red lobsters, we paddled back to the boat. The heavy-bodied grouper was red and black, but a grouper can change color to match its background.

Living off Mother Ocean's bounty was a mixed blessing. Although I enjoyed a meal of fresh fish, it was difficult to see a magnificent grouper speared and killed. I could not watch. The fish were sacred to me, and it hurt to know they must hide to be safe. The food chain seems so unfair—having to survive by eating other living things, or perhaps we're meant to eat God's flesh!

Joe fell asleep while I washed the dishes. Since it was dark, I used *Y-Not*'s spreader lights. When I threw the dish water away a small gray squid with a round body and folded tentacles darted backwards. It was too dark to see if it discharged inky fluid in self-defense. Sitting alone in the darkness, I reflected on how squid and octopi communicate with light and color and are one of the most intelligent of the invertebrates. Tired but content, I was rocked to sleep by the gentle lapping of water against the boat's belly and the rise and fall of the tide.

There were nine boats in our anchorage on March 7. Following a trail through scrubby woods on one of the islands, we found the remains of a look out tower and cistern. Birds fed on scraps of oranges and apples left on picnic tables scattered among the trees. A red and black scaly dragon-like iguana lazed in the sun. When it saw us it bobbed its head up and down. We watched spellbound.

The cistern water was so tasty that we came back to fill two five-gallon containers. Fresh water on the islands came from rain caught on the roofs of buildings and was stored in cisterns. Since hauling up the water with a bucket and rope was hard work, we took turns.

Joe put a handful of sunflower seeds in his mouth, chewed the seeds, and spat out a wad of shells. "How do you separate the seeds from the shells?" I asked, fascinated.

"I'll show you," Joe said putting a handful in his mouth. "You put the seeds in your cheek, shell them with your teeth and tongue, then spit out the shells." When I tried, the seeds migrated around my mouth.

"I can't spit," I said trying to eject two shells.

"You will have to learn," Joe laughed. When the art of spitting continued to elude me, I became frustrated and Joe gave up.

We sat in the cockpit after dinner. Stars studded the dark sky and a warm breeze came in puffs. Mother Ocean's lapping voice seemed old and wise, making us feel small, as if we should be silent.

Something was wrong. When I urinated at daybreak, I felt a burning sensation. Thinking I had a bladder infection, I began treating myself with antibiotics. Since the expiration date had passed, I did not know if they would help. I had been afraid I'd not been drinking enough liquid as I did not care for the salty taste of Nassau's desalinated water. Joe was concerned when I told him.

After lunch we had an easy downwind sail south for five miles to Allen's Cay. There were six boats in the anchorage, not the twenty we expected. Wading to the beach with our snorkel gear, we were greeted by five large iguanas. They hissed while lumbering behind us, opening and closing their mouths. We stopped to watch. It was a comfort to know that these ancient endangered lizard-like animals are protected by law.

The breeze felt pleasant when I sat in the shaded cockpit under a blue tarp on March 9, a sunny windless day. A dove's soft "coo-coo" sound echoed the gently lapping of waves while the dragon-like iguanas darted and chased each other across the beach.

Since I felt wretched, Joe went paddling alone. His easy-going, nurturing manner and his jokes and stories helped me feel more positive and to focus on the present.

Joe returned with ten pink and white foot-long conch shells containing large carnivorous mobile snails from Little Allen's Cay. The beautiful pear-shaped conchs with their pointed spires and knobbed whorls are the largest in the snail family. The soft mantle of the edible conch secretes the shell which increases in size as the animal grows.

While Joe cleaned and pounded the conch to tenderize it, a giant triangular-shaped ray jumped out of the water about fifty feet from us. Its dark arched body and whip-like tail hovered in the air before it returned to the water with a loud splash. We stood riveted on the cockpit seats as it drifted away.

The pain from my bladder infection grew worse in the evening. Tears came to my eyes. "What's wrong, hon?" Joe asked, looking concerned. He massaged my shoulders and neck to ease the pain.

After a good night's sleep I felt better in the morning. With the wind behind us we sailed three miles south to Highbourne Cay, but the cramps and burning had returned by the time we arrived.

Joe went bone fishing and I took aspirin and lay down. The hurt began to ease, but I dreaded going to the toilet. My expired antibiotics did not seem to be helping. When Joe returned he told me he had called his sister and Karen, his ex-girlfriend. "How are they?" I asked.

"My sister and her husband are excited about joining me in Georgetown. They've picked up their tickets." He paused lowering his eyes, "Karen's not doing well," he stammered. "It's not gotten through that we've broken up."

The next morning the burning in my bladder grew worse, and I had little energy. The screaming northwest wind churned up the ocean and blew all day.

The weather forecast on March 11 called for thirty-to forty-knot winds starting on March 12. Joe, and the other skippers, put out extra anchor lines and moved their boats up the channel to avoid being blown ashore. One captain wrapped his anchor line around a tree to secure his boat.

"The chemical toilet's full," Joe told me after lunch. "We need to use the bucket until it's emptied at sea."

"Oh no! Using the chemical toilet with a bladder infection is hard enough," I groaned.

The winds did not materialize on March 12 or 13 as predicted. We motored south in the bay for two hours to Norman's Cay, and emptied the chemical toilet. The sewerage left a brown trail before it was absorbed into the ocean. Feeling guilty, I wondered how much longer the ocean could assimilate our waste. Untreated sewage is pouring into the sea from many countries, cruiseships and yachts. The industrial effluents, radioactive wastes and domestic sewage may eventually kill the ocean's phytoplankton, which produce more than half the world's oxygen and provide food for fish.

At the entrance of Norman's Cay, Joe's trolling line went taut. "Stop the boat; I think we've got a fish!" he yelled. With the gears in neutral, we drifted with the tide. His line went rigid. "I'm hooked on coral," he moaned. Putting on his snorkel and mask, he grabbed his spear and dove overboard. "It's a huge grouper! It looks around eighteen pounds," he declared smiling. "It's in a hole in the coral about eight feet down." He dove again and emerged with a huge, speared, mottled brown grouper.

"How do we get it in the boat?" I asked looking around.

"Do you need help?" volunteered a dark, slender man in a French accent.

"Please," Joe responded. Between Joe and the man, they heaved the fish into the man's dinghy. It was strange how people appeared when we needed help.

"I'm Francois and I'm from the boat, *Chebec*," the man said, shaking Joe's hand. Joe invited Francois for dinner. Since he was with his wife and a friend, we suggested taking the food to their forty-five-foot sailboat.

We anchored with twelve other boats in Normans Bay. A large twin-airplane lay in waist-deep water within view. The plane remained from a time when the island had been shut down because it was used by cocaine drug dealers and corrupt police. A policeman continued to live in the area to ensure safety. The island had an airport runway and two hangars with small planes that were still in operation.

Joe grilled the grouper, and we had delightful evening with Francois and his crew.

On March 14 the sky was gray. High winds whipped up the water to make white caps and foam. Since the bay was shallow and protected by the hills, the waves were too small to rock the boat.

Later in the morning, we sailed to the Norman's Cay beach in the Klepper and met Bob and Rita. They were on *Patchy Fog*, a thirty-foot sailboat with Amanda, their two-year-old daughter; Charlie Brown, their dog; and Fluffy, their cat. While Rita talked, I played peek-a-boo with Amanda, who hid behind Rita's legs and giggled. "I had Amanda at thirty-nine, when Bob retired. She started sailing when she was ten days old," Rita said beaming. "It's great being a full time parent." They were from Clearwater, Florida. Leaving the *Patchy Fog* crew on the beach, we followed a well-used trail up the hill to the remnants of an old hotel.

After dinner Joe read me a story from his book called *Wizards and Witches*. "The story is about the dark side of life," I exclaimed and asked about his spiritual beliefs. He said he was raised a Catholic and liked to attend mass.

"To beat the blues I went to a couple of churches while kayaking in the Caribbean," Joe said wistfully. "After mass on Canouan Island, a priest followed me down to the beach to bless my kayak, and in Dominica, a priest interrupted the services to ask the parishioners to pray for my journey. I think the prayers saved me," Joe said gravely. "When I made landfall I played "Amazing Grace" on my harmonica to give thanks."

On Sunday we packed a picnic lunch, kayaked around the bay and snorkeled the entrance to Norman's Cay. While we were snorkeling two gigantic diamond-shaped black and white spotted whip rays glided through the water between the islands. Unconcerned, they swam back and forth in front of us, their whip-like tails and bodies, flapping gracefully like wings. Stirred by their presence we floated motionless and gaped. We snorkeled back to the boat and I reflected on how rays channel plankton-filled water into their vast rectangular mouth for food.

We went to get water at the hotel cistern at Norman's Cay and talked with an older balding man from *Sundown*, a black fifty-foot sailboat. The captain stopped at our boat to invite us for cocktails. "Can we take a rain check? We're really tired," Joe responded, looking at me. The skipper looked at Joe's sailboat, the two kayaks, and the rubber dinghy.

"What, you can't make up your mind!" he teased.

Although I was fatigued, my health was returning. Joe told me more stories from his Caribbean adventures. "The minister of tourism and other officials in Grenada thought I was crazy and would never make it to Puerto Rico." Joe chuckled. "Many times on the voyage I almost proved them right. I was incredibly lucky!" Joe roared with laughter when I asked what the local people were like. "When I made landfall at Grand Anse Beach at the north tip of Grenada on my first day, fifty villagers waving machetes over their heads ran down the beach. Not knowing this was a greeting, I picked up three rocks and juggled them nervously. The villagers laughed and rushed to save my kayak from the pounding surf."

"So they were friendly!"

"Yeah, when I left Grand Anse Beach for the east Caribbean islands I heard a commotion off my stern. Two fisherman from the village were behind me in a small outboard. They held the kayak's padlock and chain I had brought from New York to ward off theft. I'd inadvertently left it on the beach. I felt foolish that these honest men had gone to such trouble to return a symbol of the paranoia many Americans feel when traveling in foreign lands. The next day I deep sixed the lock and chain and left my kayak in remote and in busy places for days at a time, secured only by lines for errant tides and winds."

"In facing the elements you strengthened your faith," I said thoughtfully. "That's why you're less fearful than most of us!"

"You really understand me," Joe said in his slow, considered way.

On Monday we had a four-hour sail downwind to Warderick Wells, a hundred-and-seventy-six square mile land and sea park. The area was set aside by the Bahamas National Trust as a preserve for land and sea animals. Anchoring near the park headquarters, we attended a lecture at the cabin. Peggy, a ranger from England in her sixties, gave an informative talk on lizards and turtles in her English accent. She lived on a tug boat called *Moby* and planned to retire soon.

After breakfast we sailed the sea kayak two miles south in light winds to Loyalist beach and hiked Pegg's Trail to Rendezvous. The trail took us through tunnels of woods, across coral, and over hills with views of the ocean.

Since no spear fishing is allowed in the park, the reef was teeming with life. Tropical fish, huge friendly reddish-brown lobster and spotted grouper hovered and swam around us while we snorkeled. The hard outer shells of the ten-legged, two-clawed spinney lobster protect them from predators but also make them less mobile and flexible. Their excellent flavor is a perpetual threat to their numbers, which in many areas have been sharply reduced.

A small gray heart-shaped ridley turtle floated across the staghorn coral heads and faded into the ocean's blue depths. I'm told that for many years the breeding of this turtle remained a mystery as no nests, eggs, pregnant females or hatchlings had been found. However, we now know that large numbers lay their eggs on two beaches in Costa Rica during the months of August through November. Every year, the adult female of most turtles, having mated at sea, must leave the safety of the ocean to lay about a hundred eggs on dry land. It was fascinating to learn that turtles are the descendents of the land-living, air-breathing tortoises and date back to the age of the dinosaur two hundred and fifty million years ago.

Heading into a stiff twenty-knot wind against the tide, we were exhausted when we finally got back to *Y-Not*.

"Help! help!" cried a man. We dashed on deck and gasped. *Cast Off*, a forty-foot sailboat was adrift and about to collide with *Y-Not*. A red-faced man and a pale-looking women had their hands out to lessen the impact. Pushing against *Cast Off*, we had difficulty holding her heavy hull at bay. My heart beat faster. Joe's white sea kayak hung where *Cast Off* threatened to hit. The red-faced man and the woman bent double across their boat's pulpit while they shoved. Their eyes were wide with alarm. The man kept saying, "I'm sorry!, I'm sorry!"

"It's okay," Joe nodded furiously. "Keep pushing."

"Can I help?" volunteered a dark-haired man. He too started heaving against their boat.

"My anchor line is around your propeller!" Joe shouted. Grabbing his snorkel and mask he dove into the water. Resurfacing he exclaimed, "We're free!" *Cast Off* floated past and stopped a hundred feet down the channel before her anchor held.

The red-faced man continued to holler, "I'm sorry!"

"Don't worry!" Joe said laughing.

"I'm David," the dark-haired man introduced himself, shaking our hands. "Is this man for real?" he asked plopping down next to me. Turning to Joe, his face grew sober. "How come you don't get upset? There must be something pathological about you!"

"It's only stuff!" Joe gave a belly laugh. "On a solo kayaking expedition, I realized our lives are more important than things," he explained. David raised his eyebrows and looked impressed. He told us about himself. "I'm traveling with my wife and twelve-year-old son on our boat, *Altaire*. My wife is a lawyer and I just finished my residency as a physician. Before that, I was a nurse."

After dinner Joe read more from the *Wizards and Witches* book. One of the characters died a painful death. "I'd like to die in my sleep," I said firmly.

Joe's eyes widened. "Oh! I want to be awake and not miss it."

At sunrise we sailed the Klepper north to the Boo Boo trail to see where sailors had left the names of their sailboats. Hundreds of shells, driftwood, and other artifacts covered a hill bearing the information.

When we returned, Joe repaired the navigation lights and the tiller while I sanded and oiled *Y-Not's* woodwork. Joe accidentally stepped in some oil I'd spilled. "Shit!" he growled.

"I'm sorry!" I groaned, feeling sheepish.

"It's okay; we all make mistakes!" Joe said softly.

"I've never heard you curse before,"

He paused, "Really, I guess I try not to."

"You're so good, I feel inadequate!" I mused. "If I'm not sick, I'm spilling something, or the stove won't work."

"Yeah, my sister tells me the same thing. When I told her I have problems too, she jumped all over me, 'What, your boat's not fast enough?'" Joe laughed but looked sad. He fascinated me with his relaxed approach to life, his quick laughter and kindness.

"You're encouraging me to stay sick when you're so kind," I chided.

Not knowing whom I would be sailing with in April had begun to bother me. My instinct was that Walt, the communications professor from *Adele-T*, would not be a compatible sailing companion.

We left Wardrick Wells for a seventeen-mile sail south to Staniel Cay on March 18 but had to tack five miles west to sail with the strong southwesterly winds. When the wind died after a couple of hours, we motor-sailed in an easy swell. Perched on the bow, I reveled in the feel of the breeze.

A bluff dotted with houses overlooked the bay of our anchorage near Thunderbolt Cave around the corner from Staniel Cay village. When the wind picked up the boat rolled and bobbed in the waves, making it difficult to sleep that night. Since it was still windy in the morning, we moved the boat farther up the channel between Big and Little Major Cays. At first two boats shared our anchorage, but by nightfall we had eight boats.

After anchoring we sailed the Klepper to Staniel Cay to buy groceries. While we were buying groceries, Ray a blonde-haired man in his thirties from *Sea Lady* and his friends, Phil and Tammy, from *September Song*, approached us. Joe had traveled with Ray and Phil before. They had motored together down the Intercoastal Waterway from New York in November.

"You're a sailboat gypsy, like me," I told Tammy, Phil's tanned lithe partner, for her story was similar to mine.

Later in the afternoon, we put on our wet suits, for the water was still cold, and sailed the Klepper to *Sea Lady* to snorkel Thunderbolt cave with Ray, Phil and Tammy. Three holes in the summit of the cave let in enough light to enable us to see the coral and tropical fish. Delivered from gravity and with skin aflame from the icy water, I flew around in the silent, watery space. Schools of large black and yellow sergeant majors hovered in front of my mask, opening and closing their mouths.

Colonies of brightly colored elephant ear and tube sponges, with cells that can filter water for food and regenerate when broken, decorated the coral. Like star fish the coral are animals pulsating with life. When I touched the tube worms and mollusks they retracted their long spiral casing. A bright green, blue and yellow queen angel fish looked on inquisitively. The reef teemed with small sea anemones that divide to form their own siblings, sea urchins, sea shells and crabs. The caves looked like enormous magical castles with gardens. Buoyed by the weightlessness, I felt transfigured.

Back on *Sea Lady*, Ray gave us a tour of his boat. When he heard I was looking for another boat, he volunteered his.

"That would be great!" I said with relief.

There was a strange light that looked like a fire on the beach that night. We went to bed wondering what it was. A northerly wind made the channel choppy during the night, and the boat rolled and rattled. The next day, we moved *Y-Not* farther up the channel to lessen the surge. The wind made the white caps flit across the waves.

"I see kayaks," Joe exclaimed with a look of delight. Three dot-like figures moved towards us close to shore. Joe paddled over to invite the kayakers for pancakes. The three brothers from Chicago had been out a week and were heading for Norman's Cay to a catch a charter plane to Nassau. We had seen their fire on the beach the night before.

On Sunday we packed the camping gear in the Klepper for a two-night, kayak-camping expedition. We sailed north for three miles to Twin Cays with a blustering wind on our tail. The sun went into hiding behind the clouds. The deserted island with palm trees and a white sandy beach became our next camp. Lazing on the sand with the wind in our faces, we felt at peace.

At dawn we headed north to Sampson and Compass Cays. When a howling northerly wind and a stubborn current kept us from making headway through the cut at Compass Cay, we turned around and set up the tent farther south next to a bluff on Thompson Cay. Perched on the cliff's summit, we sat mesmerized by the after-glow of the sunset and the ocean's waves exploding against the coral.

Around midnight a storm burst over us, and it was still pouring the next morning. Getting up between squalls we paddled south in the wind-whipped rain. During one deluge, when a cold driving rain blotted out the world, I discovered my light-weight rainsuit was no longer waterproof. Soaked and shivering from cold, I was grateful that the shrieking wind behind us made for a quick return. High winds churned up the bay and rolled the boat all night, making it difficult to sleep.

On Monday I awoke with stomach cramps and discovered I had another bladder infection. Feeling tired and disappointed, I began taking the remainder of my antibiotics. We topped off the water and gas at Staniel Cay village that evening to head south to Big and Little Farmer's Cay in the morning. Since we were due in Georgetown in five days, I checked my passport and gulped. My Bahamian visa expired on the March 28, the day we would arrive. I had visions of being fined, or worse, deported or put in jail.

CHAPTER 14

A COLD FRONT

"We" are the Nature we abuse....Be gentle with your humanness. It is a privilege to be human, an honor. Man is infinite, not on a physical scale, but in Spirit.

Michael J. Roads

We are literally stars thinking about ourselves....We can't have our life, or nourishment, or learning except as it comes out of the earth, which is our very body....We're the Earth, with consciousness, with soul, with spirit. We're the Earth in a new form....If the oceans do become toxic, then the clouds are going to be toxic, and the rain will be toxic, and the corn will be toxic. And our children will be toxic, and their tears will be toxic.

Miriam Therese MacGillis

A howling twenty five-knot wind came from the direction we were going in on Wednesday, March 25. "Let's go anyway," Joe said, studying the chart. "We'll motor on the bay side. It's more protected." White caps and foam covered the gray, savage water. I felt apprehensive. The boat shuddered and slammed into six-foot waves, and the cold ocean spray stung our faces. When the wind's whine rose to a scouring roar, we bounced, heeled and banged into each wave, bronco-style. Joe was at the tiller; his face looked grim. "We've been out about two hours and we're not making headway. We'll have to turn back!" The wind was making so much noise I could hardly hear him.

"Are there other anchorages nearby?" I yelled, reluctant to return.

"Get them charts and look!" he hollered. Sliding in next to him, I pored over the charts. Joe looked over my shoulder.

"What about Bitter Guana Cay?" I inquired, pointing to a nearby island. Joe studied the chart while I held the bucking tiller until my knuckles turned white.

"Yeah, them cliffs should protect us from the wind." Joe sighed.

Turning the boat in a northeasterly direction made the motoring smoother, and we quickly approached the uninhabited island. "What beautiful cliffs!" I said looking up at the towering white jagged bluffs.

Exhausted and in pain from the bladder infection, I flopped around and slept while Joe baked bread. Feeling sick, I went to bed after dinner. During the night the wind shifted to the south, creating swells. In spite of the boat's rolling and weathering two squalls, I slept well.

At dawn we moved the boat closer to the south shore but found no protection from the surge. Studying the charts again, we looked for another sheltered anchorage. "What about Harvey Cay?" I suggested.

"You're right!" Joe grinned broadly. He narrowed his eyes and softened his voice. "I've never been with a girl like you. You make good suggestions!"

"Really!" I said, surprised. Going to Harvey Cay meant back-tracking three miles, but it was downwind and a quick sail across the rolling waters. Two small islands with a house and airstrip shielded us from the southwest wind at Harvey Cay. The wind seemed to be rotating clockwise, and we expected a northerly wind the following day.

Our suspicions were confirmed at daybreak. Reflected sunlight careened towards us when we prepared to sail the thirty-five miles south to Lee Stocking Island. Because the wind was light, and we were running out of time, Joe recommended we sail on the ocean side. The northeasterly wind strengthened, creating rough seas. Joe surveyed the white caps with a furrowed brow, then studied the chart again. "I've changed my mind; let's sail on the bay side. It'll be calmer." We sailed across the bay with a moist wind buffeting our faces. When the wind settled, we motored through Rudder Cut and rocked back and forth on choppy seas.

We arrived at Lee Stocking Island later that afternoon. A gray-haired older couple stopped to tell us we could go ashore. "There's a weather research station, and they don't mind visitors," said the man. We thanked them and kayaked to the island. A young marine mechanic from Alaska with a toothy smile showed us metal tanks containing different sized mottled grouper.

On Saturday, March 28 we left Lee Stocking Island and started to motor the twenty-two miles south to Georgetown. Following the shallow blue transparent water of the inter-island passage for nine miles, we passed white sandy beaches and small grassy hills. We motored through the cut at Soldier Cay and sailed the last thirteen miles on the ocean side. The restful rolling three-foot waves gently rocked us to and fro. At Elizabeth Harbor in Georgetown we anchored near the Peace and Plenty Hotel. Elizabeth Harbor is located between Georgetown's Great Exuma Cay and Stocking Island about a mile off-shore.

I checked with immigration about renewing my expired tourist visa, and to my dismay, found the office closed. A sign said it was open on Mondays, Wednesdays and Fridays from ten to twelve noon. Since it was Saturday, I called the number for immigration. "You have a three-day grace period," said a man with a Bahamian accent. I was relieved.

We left Georgetown's anchorage to spend the night at Stocking Island. To our surprise, Eddie stood holding an anchor line on *Luna-Sea*'s bow. His lips were pressed tight. Slowing down, I waved and yelled. He furrowed his brow and slowly lifted his hand.

"Are you heading out?" Joe asked.

"Yeah, I'm going to Conception Island tomorrow and then the Dominican Republic," he drawled.

"I need to look for Ray," I said anxiously when we anchored in the first of three lagoons since. Since Joe was expecting his sister on April 3, I hoped to sail with Ray. Stocking island was long and narrow, with hilly ridges.

Using Joe's binoculars I searched through the forest of masts of over fifty boats. *Sea Lady* was visible in the second lagoon.

When we paddled over, Ray was sitting in the cockpit. He helped us climb on board. "Darryl and I are heading to the Virgin Islands in a few days," he declared looking at me. "You're invited."

"I was hoping to get a ride back to the States," I said thoughtfully. "Let me think about it." When Darryl and Tammy arrived with towels we joined them for a swim on Stocking Island.

"We're going to do the Mona Passage between the Dominican Republic and Puerto Rica," Ray elaborated while body surfing the waves. "It's notoriously dangerous. The bottom of the ocean is lined with ship wrecks!" Ray said, tightening his jaw. "Getting through the area separates the old salts from the novices."

Since I had no desire to be an old salt, I told Ray, "I'd better find another boat or fly home."

"I understand," he said softly, then looked up and scratched his head. "I know someone who needs crew and is going back to the States," he volunteered while walking back. "I'll take you to meet him tomorrow." The skipper's name was Ike Milner and his thirty-eight-foot Endeavor was named *Osprey*.

Since Ike's boat was anchored at Kidd's Cove near Georgetown, we moved the boats after breakfast. Ray and I motored to *Osprey* in the brilliant sunshine around noon, but Ike was not in. Ray looked around the bay but did not see him. "What's he like?" I asked.

"He's got money but hides it like most rich people," Ray said wistfully. Ray and his friends were operating on a shoestring. They sailed while they had money but worked on boats or in boat yards to earn more.

"Some folks are independently wealthy and some are independently poor!" I chuckled.

"Yeah," Ray sighed.

"We'll try again later. I think Ike will be perfect for you," he said when he dropped me off at *Y-Not*. Ray was another of my guardian angels, along with Gaylin, Heinz and a long list of others. Since we were anchored nearby, I watched *Osprey* from Joe's boat. A tall, dark-haired, olive skinned, bearded man in his mid forties rowed up in a fiberglass dinghy.

I paddled over. "Hello!" I yelled, trying to slow my heartbeat. An intense looking, hawk-eyed face appeared around the awning. "Hi! Ray said you were looking for crew," I stammered.

"Yeah, come aboard," he said adjusting the ladder. Two bicycles and a small yellow surfboard were tied to the boat railing near the ladder. His brown eyes surveyed me while we introduced ourselves. "This is Smudge," he said pointing to a white cat with gold and black blotches. After sniffing my outstretched hand, she allowed me to rub her neck.

"I'm planning to take my time going back to the States. We'll go via Eleuthera and Grand Bahama Island." He paused briefly to lick his lips. "It'll take about two months." The boat looked huge compared to Joe's. Teak wood gave the cabin a warm homey atmosphere, and the brass door knobs and handles shone. Ike sat on a bunk next to a large teak table bolted to the bow floor. He propped his feet up on the table.

"I love your boat!" I exclaimed plopping down opposite him.

"Yeah, she's a good old gal," he said smiling. "Come to Daddy," he cooed gathering Smudge in his arms. Leaning forward he said, "I'm waiting for my dinghy's outboard engine. I sent it to Nassau to get fixed ten days ago, and I don't know when it will be back."

"I'm interested in sailing with you," I blurted, surprised at my quick decision.

"That's fine!" He smiled.

"I'd like to come aboard on April 3, when Joe's sister arrives."

"No problem! We got up. Do you sing?"

"No," I said scrunching up my face.

"Too bad, I'm a singer."

"Really? What kind of music?"

"Blues."

Ray stopped by shortly after I returned. "Let's try Ike again."

"I've met him," I said brightly.

"Oh," he muttered sounding disappointed. "Are you going with him?"

"Yes. You're an angel; thanks for putting us in touch."

It was a relief to have found another boat. Feeling sad about leaving Joe, I was glad we had four more days together.

"I'll miss you," Joe said teary-eyed when he heard about my decision to sail with Ike. Tears came to my eyes also. "Traveling with you was the best," he said gazing at me.

Joe took me out to eat at the Two Turtles Resort. Walt, the retired communications professor from *Adele-T*, joined us for part of the dinner.

"I'm disappointed you've found another boat," he said sternly.

On Monday, the immigration office extended my Bahamian visa for another two months. There was a line at the post office when I stopped to pick up my mail. I stated my name at the counter and an elderly man tapped me on the shoulder. "I saw your ad in Nassau to crew the day after you left." He smiled. "I can take you." His boat's name was *Born Free*, and he was heading for the Virgin Islands. Thanking him, I explained I already had a boat.

I called Wayne. "I'm glad you called," he sighed. "I've been concerned about you." I checked with your friends and they hadn't heard from you either."

"I'm sorry. I didn't mean to get you worried."

Wayne became business like. "Your house insurance was canceled since you're not living in the house. I went to the company's office, but they wouldn't renew and returned your check."

"Thanks! I'll straighten it out when I get back. I'll be returning on June 1."

"Good. I'll move out May 30."

Georgetown, the capital of the Exumas, is a quaint village with no traffic lights and a huge evergreen tree in the town square. We were told the harbor had four hundred boats for the Out Island Regatta that year. The majority of native-born Exumans are descendents of the slaves of English and Irish plantation managers. Farming and fishing sustained the Exumas until the tourist industry began to grow.

On Tuesday, Joe and I paddled to Crab Cay to snorkel. The snorkeling was disappointing as the water was murky from overuse. The following morning we sailed two hours south to Red Shanks Cay and anchored with seven boats in a shimmering bay surrounded by uninhabited hilly islands. The peace and silence of the bay were a welcome replacement to the hustle and bustle of Kidds Cove.

The huge red ball of the setting sun highlighted pink, yellow and gold crests on the breakers at dusk. "I dreamed about you last night," Joe said turning to me. "A man grabbed your arm and tried to kiss you at a restaurant."

"What did you do?"

"I punched him!" Joe said with a faint look of amusement. His dream made me feel warm inside. We had come to care for each other, but the timing was wrong. We were evidently destined to be friends, not lovers.

We returned to Kidds Cove in the afternoon. Dave, his son, and Ike were leaving in a rubber dinghy to spear fish. "I'll see you at ten tomorrow," I yelled to Ike. He nodded.

Joe went to town to call his sister at dusk. I sat on *Y-Not's* bow to watch the sea mirror Georgetown's twinkling lights. The smell of salt spray wafted through the air. Although my heart was heavy about leaving Joe, my sadness dissipated like vapor when he returned.

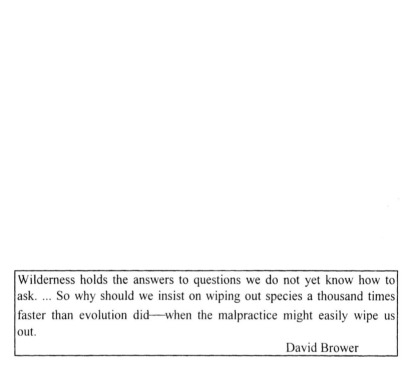

Wilderness holds the answers to questions we do not yet know how to ask. ... So why should we insist on wiping out species a thousand times faster than evolution did—when the malpractice might easily wipe us out.

David Brower

CHAPTER 15

OSPREY

We are the consciousness of the earth. These are the eyes of the earth. And this is the voice of the earth.

Joseph Campbell

The gray, rainy morning of April 3 matched my mood. I wept when Joe transferred me to *Osprey*, and left Kidds cove to anchor in the main channel.

Ike went spear fishing, but feeling fragile I stayed on the boat. He returned at five o'clock and invited me to dinner at the Two Turtles Hotel. When it began to pour we changed our minds. Instead, Ike cooked the grouper he caught earlier and combined it with crab meat. The rain was so heavy, his boat collected eighty gallons of water in one hour when the deck funnelled the rain-water into two water tanks.

Sitting at the teak table after dinner, we exchanged our life stories. Ike grew up in New Hampshire. His parents were in the hotel business. "My sister and I were raised by nannies during the summer months," he groaned. "To make a living I fixed up old houses. *Osprey* was bought with the money from one of the houses," he said proudly.

This was Ike's second extended sailing trip with a girlfriend. "They said they missed being on land and left halfway through the trips," Ike complained. "Susan left two weeks ago after six months," he remarked, rubbing Smudge's neck. He cleared his throat. "The people I love leave. It happened in my childhood, and it happens now!"

"That's been the story of my life too," I nodded. "My parents were also absent."

Ike's face darkened, "I was married once for a number of years. It was a disaster." His eyes narrowed. "She was destitute and had two kids. After we married she turned into a bitch; I could do nothing right," he said fiercely. "So much for social work!"

"I'm sorry!"

"Yeah!" He shrugged. Ike closed his cabin door for the night and I made a bed out of a bunk in the bow.

In the morning, Ike limped out of his cabin groaning and squinting. "Did someone get the license plate of the bus that ran over me?" he moaned. "My arthritis flared-up and I didn't get any sleep."

The rain stopped around noon but the clouds and haze remained. It took awhile to learn to row Ike's fiberglass dinghy, but I did get to Georgetown and back to buy groceries.

"My heritage is Jewish, but that's where it ends. I'm an atheist," Ike stated that evening. He had strong feelings about South Africa. "Too bad they no longer have apartheid. It worked."

"How can you say that?" I said horrified.

"Look at the other African countries that have black governments. They're a mess, economically and politically," he countered.

"Apartheid is not the solution," I snapped. "The blacks were exploited; they had no family life, no assets, no rights." He shrugged and rolled his eyes. We realized our values were worlds apart; to get along we'd have to agree to disagree. However, I appreciated his willingness to debate.

We prepared to sail south to Red Shanks at first light. After stowing the gear, I motored the boat forward while Ike pulled up the anchor. Remembering how I lost control of Joe's boat the first day, I was relieved when all went well. Squinting into the sun's glare we anchored at Red Shanks.

A two-foot long silver torpedo-shaped barracuda trailed us while we snorkeled. Its sleek body moved with grace as it pensively patrolled the reef. My skin turned to gooseflesh. Two rows of needle sharp teeth were visible when it opened and closed its long jutting jaws. It swam off into the twilight.

Swimming among the red and orange coral heads, I marvelled how the spots, stripes and dappled markings of the fish helped disguise their presence. The tail end of a black-and-white striped butterfly fish had a large black dot inside a white circle while its real eye was obscured by a black vertical line. It swam backwards, making the false eye seem more real. When a larger fish lunged towards it, the butterfly fish switched directions and vanished. Suspended in the silent watery world, I watched spellbound.

After snorkeling we rowed to a beach where people left boat names on conch shells. Since boaters gathered there for drinks or cookouts, it was named the "Red Shanks Tennis Club." Ike later printed the boat's name on a conch shell for the Club, and showed it to me. It read, "**Boat *Osprey*, Ike, Niki and Smudge**." His including me felt good.

Y-Not sailed by while we were having lunch on deck. Joe, his sister and brother-in-law waved. I felt my face go warm. "We're waiting for good weather to sail south," Joe yelled before anchoring up the cove. He took his family to the happy hour at the "Tennis Club" that evening.

"Why were we not invited?" Ike moaned while making pizza.

"It's an open invitation," I explained. Looking down, he kneaded the dough with vigor. The Tennis Club gathering broke up an hour later.

"Joe is fascinating. He doesn't get angry," I told Ike.

Ike rolled his eyes and grinned. "You can't say that about me. I turn the air purple!" His face hardened. "You talk a lot about Joe!" When I inadvertently mentioned Joe again, Ike declared, "I'm sick of hearing about Joe." I sat in stunned silence.

After dinner Ike fingered his guitar absently. The chords swelled and died before drifting together to form a number of blues songs. He added his keyboard-synthesizer and started to sing in a deep rich voice. His voice shimmered with energy, and I smiled with pure pleasure. I could not pull my eyes away from his face, which glowed with something soft, but also wild. "You sing like an angel!" I said, astonished.

It suddenly seemed to me we had a lot in common; we shared a love for animals, we felt strongly about conserving the earth's resources and had little use for American politics.

On Monday, we spent another night at Red Shanks, sheltered from the cold wind and choppy waves.

"Who's the glorious chairman of the Chinese Peoples' Republic?" Ike asked Smudge when he emptied a can of cat food in her bowl.

"Meow!"

"Mao! That's right," Ike chuckled. "Aren't you a smart little mouser!" Quizzing Smudge was part of his morning routine. "My humor can be abrasive," Ike said over breakfast. "Let me know if I hurt your feelings."

Joe's boat was gone at dawn. We rowed to Crab Cay to hike a trail to the hilltop ruins. Silver streaks of sunlight gleamed on the ocean when we sat on one of the ruin walls. Tiny yellow birds flitted among the trees that cast sun-dappled shadows on the earth. Ike looked at me and started to say something but stopped. When I glanced at him, his eyes softened. "I think I'm falling in love with you," he whispered. He looked down, "I've never felt this way!" he said hoarsely.

My face felt warm. "I feel close to you, too," I sighed.

Ike brightened. "You mean I have a chance?"

"Of course!"

"I've been obsessed with you ever since we met. I watched you with my binoculars," Ike confessed. "I nearly called the whole thing off. You're too attractive and it would be torture sailing with you," he said plaintively.

"I'm glad you didn't," I chuckled.

We left Red Shanks on Tuesday. Although the anchorage was choppy at Kidds Cove, we stayed to buy groceries and run errands.

Joe called us on the VHF radio and invited us to go fishing on Wednesday. Ike declined, but I accepted. Joe, Bill and Michelle picked me up at noon. "What do you think of sailing?" I asked Joe's sister.

"It's been tough," Michelle moaned, shaking her short dark hair. "With the boat bouncing and rolling we've not slept and we're not used to such cramped quarters." Feeling awkward about leaving Ike, I was glad to get back to *Osprey*. That evening we sat in the bow holding hands and gazing into each others' eyes.

The dinghy's outboard engine arrived the following day, so we were free to sail north. Joe stopped to say good-bye in the afternoon. A local couple agreed to watch Joe's boat at Stocking Island when he returned to work in the States. "Michelle and Bill slept at a hotel last night," Joe said grinning. "They couldn't handle living on a boat."

Since strong winds came from the direction we were heading on Friday, Ike moved *Osprey* to Stocking Island, to wait for better weather. It felt natural to move into Ike's tiny cabin that night. To my horror, mounted to the wall above the bunk was a pistol.

"Do you need a gun?" I asked surprised, for neither Eddie nor Joe carried one.

"I almost had to use it at Little Farmer's Cay when some guys boarded my boat," Ike snorted. "When they saw the gun they took off."

Because the northerly wind was still blowing on Sunday, we stayed another day. At a pot-luck on Volleyball Beach that evening, Dave and Ike played their guitars and sang spirited sailing songs around a campfire.

On April 13 the winds were calm. We began to motor-sail the twenty-two miles north to Lee Stocking Island on the ocean side. Within two hours we were beating into an eighteen-knot wind and three-foot waves, which made our progress slow.

After we had anchored at Lee Stocking Island, Ike dove into the water to pick up some large pink and white conchs to use as bait for line fishing. He kept the conchs alive in a bag submerged in water over the side of the boat.

We held hands on deck and watched the setting sun's fiery red ball peek through gold-trimmed clouds. "Why do you always wear a shirt?" I inquired.

"I've been overweight all my life," Ike groaned. "No one is allowed to see my body!"

"You look fine. I'd be proud."

"Yeah," he said thoughtfully. "I've lost weight, but I'm still self conscious."

The next morning we walked to a deserted beach. A veil of clouds crept across the sky while I swam in the nude. After watching me swim naked, Ike entered the water without clothes and frolicked in the surf like a caged animal set free. We dressed and started back to the boat. An elderly couple wearing white peaked caps walked towards us on the trail.

"Hi, Niki!" said the man.

"How did you know my name?" I exclaimed.

"It's in the visitors' book!" The man laughed. "My wife's name is Niki." The woman smiled. "Jim's the name," the man said shaking our hands. "Would you like to come over for drinks?"

"Yeah, that's fine," Ike responded without looking at me.

We started back to the dinghy. "Ike, I don't feel up to socializing this evening," I stammered.

Ike's eyes narrowed. "Damn, I've already told them 'yes.' Can't we go for a little while?"

"I need some quiet time," I pleaded. "Why don't you go?"

He stalked off while I followed, and we motored to *Osprey* in silence. Gaylin's boat *Morning Star* was anchored in the bay. Gaylin called on the VHF radio to invite us for drinks. Ike spoke to him. "I'll call you back with an answer," he told him. He looked at me pleadingly.

"No," I said emphatically. Annoyed, Ike called Gaylin back to decline. He tried calling Jim and Niki without success. After a sharp warning look, he lay in the cabin with a book. I flopped on deck. A cold salty howling twenty-knot wind mingled with my warm salty silent tears. Pink and white storm clouds floated west and patchy rays of sunshine flickered on the foamy water. Feeling strangely comforted by the elements, I returned to Ike. He glanced up looking annoyed.

"I'm sorry I hurt you!"

His face softened and he reached to hug me.

"I'm sorry too," he said softly.

My feeling of being overwhelmed, and my need to be consulted about decisions, gushed out. He tried to call the other boat without success. "I'll go over to let them know we're not coming."

The shrieking northeasterly wind continued to blow for two days, transforming the gray bay into a raging wonderland of white caps. The rawness of the water and wind matched my mood.

On Thursday we hiked around the island again. Since it was too cold to swim we motored to the weather station and brought back thirty gallons of water in large plastic containers. The dinghy engine coughed and died on a return trip to *Osprey*. "I just got it fixed in Nassau," Ike spat trying to repair it. "I'll call the dealer when we get to Staniel Cay." He scowled while we rowed back.

We motor-sailed north in light winds for thirty miles to Staniel Cay on Friday, April 17. My spirits cleared with the weather. After anchoring off the Staniel Cay Yacht Club Ike went to call the Nassau outboard engine dealer. He returned muttering under his breath.

"We have to stop in Nassau," he complained. "I hate the place!" They promised to replace the engine if it could not be repaired.

On Sunday we sailed downwind for seventeen miles north to Wardrick Wells on the ocean. Ike caught an eight-pound tuna and he happily held the fish up for me to take a photograph. We anchored in a deserted cove with white sand and turquoise water between Wardrick Wells and Hog Island. Then we frolicked in the water while the warm sun and gentle breeze caressed our naked bodies.

Another boat, *Windsong*, arrived in the late afternoon. Ike called and offered to share his freshly caught tuna. The owners, a couple in their fifties, accepted and motored over. Afterwards Ike referred to the day on Hog Island as the best day of his life.

On Tuesday Ike gave sailing instructions while we took turns steering the twenty-two miles east in a gentle, restful swell to Eleuthera. Arriving at Powell Point, the southern tip of Eleuthera, we motored up a channel flanked with pine trees. Another sailboat, *Applied Systems*, was anchored to the left. Ike began motoring to the right.

"Jesus!" he yelled, putting *Osprey* in reverse. "We just missed hitting that anchor line!" *Applied Systems'* anchor line was wrapped around a tree on the opposite bank. Reversing the boat, he threw out the anchor.

"Damn idiots!" he muttered, then stomped across the deck and disappeared in the cabin.

Afraid of Ike's ferocity, I remained on deck and looked at the water and trees to calm down. A black rubber dinghy with a bearded red-haired man and a blonde woman aboard stopped at *Applied Systems*. Ike rushed on deck.

"What the hell were you doing, blocking the channel!" Ike roared. The woman turned white.

"I'll damn well do what I like!" the red-haired man fired back in an English accent. "You don't own this place," the man sneered, his face a bright red.

I escaped below deck, my heart pounding. Ike had said his anger "turned the air purple"—he was right! He entered the cabin looking satisfied.

We paddled to the beach and followed a path to an abandoned resort which looked like a ghost town. In the mid 1650s Bermuda exiled its troublesome slaves to Eleuthera.

Pineapples were once a chief export but by the 1940s they had fallen due to the competition from Hawaii and Cuba.

When we got back, *Applied Systems* had removed its offending anchor line. After *Applied Systems* left on Thursday, we motored up the channel to a small lake.

Because of pain when I urinated, I suspected I had another bladder infection. To my dismay, I realized my antibiotics were gone. Luckily, Ike had a course of sulfur pills. Feeling depressed and disappointed I went for a walk along a wooded trail that followed the water inlet.

Ike played his guitar, sang and did comedy routines from George Burns and Bill Cosby that evening. Ike was a good story teller and comedian. I sat enthralled and I laughed till I cried. "How do you remember the songs and lines?"

He looked at me and beamed. "My I.Q. is a hundred seventy!"

On Wednesday we sailed forty-two miles north on a beam reach to Hatchet Bay, Eleuthera and anchored near the marina. A paved road runs the hundred-mile length of Eleuthera's sickle shape, which is up to two miles in width.

That evening we had dinner at The Rainbow Inn restaurant, a two-mile walk south of the boat. Friendly truck drivers stopped to give us a ride both ways. When we got back Ike talked with Byron, a handsome black marina manager with whom he had played music at a nightclub last year.

The next day we had a picnic lunch on Eleuthera's eastern shore. High bluffs overlooked the Atlantic's waves that crashed on a beach a mile from the marina. To my relief, my bladder infection improved and my energy returned.

On Friday morning we took our washing to the laundry in Alice Town. A black woman with large, watchful eyes told us the water pressure was too low for the washing machines. The next day we followed a worn path that led to a cave entrance in a rocky hill. Our flashlights showed a path through a number of dark, cool chambers. There were a few icy white stalactites hanging from the roof, but sadly the walls were mostly covered with graffiti. Noticing a pool of light in a far chamber, we walked over and looked up. Sunlight streamed down a twenty-foot well. Feeling dizzy, I retraced my steps to the cave's entrance.

The wind came from Nassau's direction on Sunday, so we postponed our departure. Instead we walked around Alice Town listening to the echoes from church sermons and songs. I'm told most Bahamians are devout, and much of their social life is centered around the churches. The Anglican Church is the official Church of the State, but there are no religious restrictions.

After dinner Ike untied the dinghy. "I'm taking the garbage ashore," he said with a wave. When Ike had not returned after two hours, I became concerned. The water pump did not go off when I filled the kettle for tea. I switched the pump to manual and called the Marina but I got no reply. I put down my tea and stared at the empty cabin. Not being able to get to shore made me feel helpless. Since my mother had been a hospital emergency room physician, I had a tendency to think the worst. Unable to concentrate on my reading, I fidgeted and tapped my foot on the floor.

Eventually, an hour later, I heard a splash and dashed on deck. Ike rowed up with his back to me. I met him at the ladder. He looked at me and smiled archly. "I've been worried," I said in a quavering voice.

He grinned sheepishly, "I was bad; Byron bought me a drink."

"I'm glad you're safe," I snivelled.

"Sorry," Ike shrugged, looking mischievous. "I was bad."

He tried to fix the water pump but could not. "I need to get a part in Nassau," he sighed.

CHAPTER 16

WATER SPOUTS

Every creature is a word of God and a book about God.
                    Meister Eckhart

On Monday the fifteen-knot northeast wind looked good for sailing the forty-two miles west to Nassau. But the wind died after two hours so we motored most of the way. Arriving in Nassau after dark, we anchored near the Basra dock. Shortly after our arrival the wind picked up to twenty-five knots and continued to howl all night.

On Tuesday we took Ike's outboard engine and water pump to the dealers for repairs. I stopped off to do laundry. Nick, the manager at the East Bay Marina, a short black friendly fellow, recognized me.

"You're the person who placed an ad to crew," he said taking me by the arm and leading me to a large sailboat. Before I could reply he yelled, "Hey, John!" A blonde man in a dark blue T-shirt that matched his eyes appeared. Nick introduced us and left. I explained what happened. It turned out John sailed charter boats to the States for a living.

When I got back to *Osprey*, Ike had picked up and fixed the water pump. "The dealer also replaced my outboard engine," he said sounding relieved.

Later that afternoon, we strolled along the beach. Ike found a beautiful lapis lazuli beaded necklace and gave it to me. As we approached the summit of the Paradise Island arched bridge I mentioned I'd like to marry again. He stopped. "Is that a marriage proposal?" he asked gazing intently into my eyes.

"N..no," I stammered in surprise. His question made me feel warm inside.

We planned to leave Nassau on Wednesday for the thirty-seven mile sail to the Berry Islands. Pulling up the anchor at daybreak we started to motor north to Chub Cay. Twenty minutes later we were buffeted by a strong head wind. Making no headway, we turned around and headed back to Nassau. Disappointed, Ike went shopping in Nassau and I went swimming on Paradise Island.

When I walked out of the water, Ike strode up with a duffel bag over his shoulder. He spotted me and threw the bag on the beach. And then he flung his arms around my waist and kissed me hard on the lips. "I ... Ike," I groaned. Embarrassed, I glanced up. The spectators were smiling.

We returned to *Osprey* later that afternoon. "I have something for you!" Ike said, handing me a purple jewelry box. A smile flickered at the corners of his mouth.

"Emerald earrings! They're beautiful." I oohed and aahed. "Thank you," I bubbled giving him a hug. Placing the earrings in my ears, I looked in the mirror.

"Green's your color," Ike said admiringly. "I'm so glad Ray introduced us," he said with a surge of elation. He looked at the ceiling and chuckled. "Thank you, Ray!" It felt good to be spoiled.

Ike took a fresh water shower on deck. "You should've seen me in Nassau!" he chuckled. "A woman at the fruit market asked, 'You from a sailboat, man?'"

"Yeah, how did you know?

'You don't get a tan like that in a week, man!'"

We left Nassau on Saturday for the Berry Islands and motored most of the thirty-seven miles into a gentle swell. The sun was setting when we anchored near the entrance to Chub Cay Marina.

After breakfast we zipped over to Mama Rhoda Rock in the dinghy to snorkel. Large red and blue lacey fans swayed in unison among mountains of stag, elkhorn, fire and brain coral. Multi-colored fish hovered among the weeds. Unconcerned about predators, schools of fish hung before us waving their fins and tails.

A sting ray hid in the sand with only its eyes exposed. Our eyes locked. When I dove to get a closer look, it shot forward with sinuous undulations of its disc-like body. It had a long, thin pointed tail, and its two-foot-across, flat upper body was grey with a creamy white underside. A sting ray's body is supported by cartilage as rays have no bones.

Aware of being part of the food chain, I turned an occasional circle and kept a wary eye on the open water for the toothy, sleek, dark form of a shark. Pulsing bells of jelly fish that looked like liquid ghosts fed by using the tentacles on their mucous nets. A diamond-shaped brilliant blue, green and yellow queen trigger fish blew water at the sand to uncover food. I read that the trigger fish's name comes from its ability to lock itself in a crevice with its dorsal fin when a predator approaches.

Hypnotized by the fish and coral, time moved with new meaning. Snorkeling was magical—time became suspended, with only the water, fish and us.

After dinner we moved *Osprey* to the north end of Chub Cay. A twenty-knot northeast wind had made our anchorage choppy. Ike motored cautiously, for the depth sounder kept beeping, indicating that the water in the area was shallow. "I don't like this anchorage," he spat, throwing out the anchor. He snarled at me for not having more sailing experience, then retired with a book.

My face grew hot. "I'll catch a plane back tomorrow," I stammered with rage.

His eyes blazed as though I'd hit him. "No," he said, reaching for me. Although my insecurity melted, I began to wonder about our future. Our relationship had begun to feel like a roller coaster ride, and I questioned whether we would make it back to the States together.

Adapting to the lives of others on a boat was difficult; it reminded me of my childhood—living in different homes, being on my best behavior, having to leave the people I loved. How others stayed together remained a mystery. Then it hit me—in repeatedly saying goodbye to the people I loved, I'd recreated my childhood.

On Tuesday the sun was still low in the sky when we motored five miles to Little Whale Cay and anchored in a bay surrounded by hilly islands. While hiking along the bay, we paused to watch the triangular wedges of six sharks, about three feet in length, swimming where the ocean broke on a shallow beach. They churned the water in what looked like a feeding frenzy. My toes curled in my sandals.

When we returned a forty-foot trimaran named *Wings* and a three-story motor boat were anchored near *Osprey*. After dinner Bob and Sydney, a couple in their fifties from W*ings*, stopped over to invite us for drinks.

While we sipped wine with Bob and Sidney on deck at dusk a small outboard motor-boat took guests from the three-story ship to the beach. The occupants were mostly women in long white dresses. When the last of the group had been deposited, Ike called the tanned young male driver over.

"What are they doing?" he asked pointing to the beach.

"They're a metaphysical group, and they're doing a ritual to raise Atlantis!" The young man grinned.

"Oh!" Ike and the couple chuckled. Intrigued, I sat in silence.

Bob and Sydney were resort owners in Rhode Island and Florida. "We're on vacation for two weeks," Sydney explained. While we talked, the women on the beach moved around in a circle, their candles flickering like fire flies in the dark. Faint sounds of chanting and prayer mingled with the lapping water.

At daybreak Bob and Sydney sailed past us heading for Nassau. Ike talked to Bob on the radio two hours later. "We turned back. We had a twenty-five-knot wind on our nose and the seas were lumpy," he explained.

Sailing downwind we quickly covered the seven-and-a-half miles to Little Harbor Cay. We had just dropped the anchor when the howling wind moved to the south, making

Osprey bob up and down like a cork. The ocean looked gray with white patches of foam through the bay entrance.

A wall of dense black clouds moved rapidly towards us from the southwest and huge ocean swells developed in the shrieking wind. A bright white jagged sheet of lightning ripped across the darkening sky with a sudden violent crash of thunder. I jumped reflexively.

We blinked at the blackness and froze. "Oh, shit!" Ike blurted, his eyes transfixed with horror. "Water spouts!" Two large black spouts, each the width of a small house, headed towards the boat. I gawked in disbelief. The air felt charged with electricity. Ike dropped and secured the bimini top.

"What happens if we get hit?" I gulped, my heart hammering in my chest.

"I don't know," he said hoarsely, and gripped the narrow companionway until his knuckles turned white. We gazed at the spouts as if hypnotized. Extending from the ocean to the clouds, they whirled towards us, twisting like giant black snakes. White waves and spray thundered where the spouts met the ocean. A spurt of adrenaline made me want to take cover, but my body stood paralyzed.

A thunder clap shook the world, drowning out the screaming wind. Eerie streaks of lightning danced overhead. I drew in my breath and gave a startled gasp. About three car lengths from the boat the spouts separated. One moved to the right and one to the left within fifty feet. The water spouts hit the island and branches, leaves, dust and debris exploded in the air. We watched with numbed horror.

"Whew! That was close!" Ike sighed, plopping down on a cockpit seat.

"The universe looked after us," I stammered with my heart in my throat. "Thank you, Great Spirit!" I whispered in awe.

Later that afternoon we snorkeled around a small island called Cabbage Cay. Waves and water surged through an underwater tunnel. When Ike began spear fishing, I returned to *Osprey*.

Thirty minutes later I heard a splash and looked around. Ike was swimming rapidly towards the boat, his eyes wide in alarm. His face looking ashen as he scambled aboard. "A shark came after me," he gasped. "I barely escaped!"

Ike and I began to argue after dinner. We went in circles, trying to prove our points. "This is going nowhere," I grumbled, and stormed into the cabin. Ike remained on deck. The wind increased, rattling the boat. A loud banging sound came from above. My body tensed. I thumbed through a book. Two hours later, I got ready for bed. Gusts of wind roared in the rigging, and overhead the thumping and slamming intensified.

"Damn!" Ike yelled.

"Do you need help?" I shouted from the companionway. Ike's dark silhouette sat on the bow. He glanced up but did not answer. My irritation increased and I went to bed. The wind continued to howl, along with hammering sounds. A little before midnight Ike entered the cabin. His jaw was clenched and his eyes blazed.

"What's wrong?" I stammered, swallowing a lump in my throat.

"I lost a bumper overboard and had to get it. Then the boat anchor dragged and had to be relocated!" he said acidly. He lay down and sighed. The wind subsided and it became quiet.

Astonished, my skin turned to gooseflesh. "The wind gusts coincided with our fight!" I marveled.

"Huh!" Ike mumbled, then fell asleep. Wide-eyed I wondered if the wind's dying was a coincidence. Had we become a part of the universal current of life where all things are connected?

The following morning, we hiked a trail to the ocean side of Little Harbor Cay. We passed a house owned by the Darvell family, whom Ike had met last year. Ike picked through the seaweed and garbage that littered the high water mark, while I sat cross-legged contemplating the ocean's churned up waves that crashed on the beach. When we returned, Mrs. Darvell, an attractive black woman wearing a red print dress, stood in front of the house. She greeted us with a wave and agreed to sell us three pawpaws, two cabbages, and sixteen sapadillas (similar to kiwi fruit) for five dollars.

The next day, we hiked on one of Little Harbor Cay's inland trails. A red tag in the ground caught Ike's eye. He started to dig when he could not pull the tag out. A green garbage bag came into view. He dug further and found two more. The dried leaves inside looked like marijuana. We left the bags there, since neither of us smoked pot and the penalties for drug possession on a boat are severe.

The following morning, we sailed seventeen miles to Panton's Cove at Great Stirrip Cay and anchored near three beaches. Ike had found five, two-foot-long silver bars there last year and hoped to get more. He thought they might be valuable. After breakfast we snorkeled off the third beach to search for the silver bars at an old shipwreck. We found none.

On Thursday we used Ike's two bicycles to explore Great Harbor Cay under a blazing sun. The four-mile long and two-mile wide Cay is the largest island in the Berry's and has about six-hundred residents. The first known settlement, Williamstown, was built in 1836 for homeless ex-slaves. Ruins of the old customhouse are all that remain. We started at the northern end and cycled three miles to a town. A few houses dotted a flat, mostly barren, scrubby looking countryside.

We were told American Cruise Lines and a Norwegian Cruise Ship brought their passengers to picnic on the beaches over the weekends and that they did not mind sailboat visitors. We were disappointed when no cruise ship appeared on Friday. While hiking after lunch we spotted a Norwegian cruise ship transporting its tourists to the beach in small boats. We joined them for left-over hamburgers, hot dogs, and barbecued chicken later that afternoon.

I sat on the beach to watch the setting sun turn the water shades of pink and gold. "Are you contemplating the Infinite?" Ike inquired. "You watch the water for hours." It was true. Perhaps chromosomes and forgotten memories explain why I gaze at the sea with such yearning.

On Monday, the day we planned to leave for Freeport, a twenty-five-knot wind came from the wrong direction.

"We can't sail to Lucaya in that!" Ike said, rolling his eyes. "We'll have to wait."

CHAPTER 17

EGO DEATH

And you shall bless darkness as you would bless light.
Kahlil Gibran

We left Great Stirrip Cay at dawn on Tuesday. A fog cast a delicate white curtain. Since there was little wind, we motored the fifty miles to Lucaya in an easy swell. Motoring up a channel at Lucaya we anchored in a lake with three other boats. A band stand, curio shops, restaurants and hotels were visible from the shore.

Grand Bahama Island is the northernmost island in the Bahamas and is seventy miles long and up to eight miles wide. Unlike downtown Freeport, which is more industrial, Lucaya is known as the garden city with its resorts, gambling casino, residential areas and white sandy beaches. During the twenty years that have followed the introduction of gambling, prosperity in Lucaya has grown.

The next morning, we took one of Ike's silver bars to the "Dive Company Salvage Store and Museum." A dark-haired, bearded man with a slight paunch, identified the bars as aluminum and not worth much.

On Thursday, Ike went gambling and won sixty dollars while I was at the beach. He used his winnings to celebrate by buying us dinner at Pusser's Restaurant that evening.

"Your voice makes my toes curl," Ike said fondly, holding my hand at the table. "I am so glad I found you." He looked up, his eyes shining with pleasure. "Thank you, Ray!" Aglow with warm feelings, I felt more hopeful about us.

Ike wanted to make the ninety-mile Gulf Stream crossing to the States on Saturday. We planned to spend our last night at West End, an abandoned resort town twenty-five miles northwest of Freeport. When a cold front and strong winds prevented us from leaving over the weekend, Ike became edgy. My sore throat turned into a cold so we stayed on the boat to bake bread and read.

On Saturday we went to see the dolphins used in the tourist shows. We hiked two miles to Sanctuary Bay in the stiff breeze. Ike walked on the road while I strolled along the beach. The dolphins were housed in a large fenced-off lagoon, so we watched through the wire from a distance. The trainers had the dolphins jump through loops, fetch balls and do other tricks for a group of admiring tourists. The dolphins' intelligence, squeaky voices and playfulness were astonishing.

Research shows that the brains of dolphins resemble human brains but are up to twenty percent larger. There are other similarities—the number of cells connected to one another, the number of layers in their cortex, and the amount of large "silent areas" for central processing of speech, vision, hearing and motor integration. Although their visual system is one-tenth the speed of ours, their sonic and acoustic systems are more complex, ten times as fast and at ten times the frequency.

I read with fascination how sea mammals' brains evolved thirty million years ago whereas our current brains are about one hundred thousand years old. Their longer evolution period may account for their highly developed sense of ethics. Records show that no dolphin has injured a human being. Even when dolphins are cruelly treated, they do not respond with violent actions. Although they can bite a five-foot fish in two with their teeth, they show remarkable forbearance with humans in the water. Playful, curious, and patient, dolphins in captivity develop close attachments to people.

It was stirring to learn that sick and grieving dolphins are cared for by other dolphins and that they will commit suicide if their incapacity becomes great enough to endanger the group. Without an automatic respiratory system like ours, a dolphin will die when unconscious unless it is brought by other dolphins to the surface to breathe.

Although fascinated with dolphins, humans continue to kill them by unregulated fisheries and purse seine fishing, and they are still drowning in the up to twenty-five thousand miles of ocean nets. Before the drive for "dolphin safe" nets, more than a quarter of a million dolphin were drowned or killed annually by tuna fisherman.

I read to my dismay that in May of 1997, the White House made a proposal to ease the dolphin safety rule and once again allow fisherman to scoop up the dolphins in the nets when they catch tuna. Under the pact fisherman would chase, catch and release dolphins as long as the boat carried independent observers who certified that no dolphins were killed. However, since dolphins have no automatic respiratory system, such a practice could cause the dolphins to suffer strokes and die later, out of sight of an on-boat observer. Dolphins can also die prematurely during their capture and from the confinement when used for human entertainment in circus-like settings.

Many people, myself included, are pleading for the cessation of industrial and commercial use of dolphins and recommending they no longer be considered as property or food. We have not yet understood all of those factors necessary for our long-term survival over the millennia. Seeing the dolphins and other animals into the next century and beyond foretells our own ecological future.

When the wind subsided on Tuesday, Ike and I motor-sailed the twenty-eight miles into a gentle breeze to West End and anchored beyond the marina with two other boats.

West End shows signs of its prosperous past enterprise selling liquor during Prohibition. The abandoned two-thousand acre Jack Tar · village, a marina, numerous warehouses and a half sunk pier dotted the shoreline.

Lazing in the cockpit I mused how the boat names on my trips seemed to reflect my experiences. *Luna-Sea* had been about loneliness and wanting to return home. *Y-Not* had been about renewed commitment, and my feelings soared and plummeted like a bird in flight on *Osprey*.

Since we planned to cross the Gulf Stream at three in the morning we went to bed early. Sleep did not come easily for either of us.

We left West End in the dark around three for Fort Pierce, a ninety-mile sail northwest of Grand Bahama Island. A tiny sliver of a moon rose out of the water at four as we motor-sailed with a five-knot wind behind us. Taking a break from my one-hour watch at the helm, I napped in the cockpit with Smudge, the cat, draped across my chest. Not having slept well the last two nights, Ike and I were both cranky. Although hazy at sunrise the deck by mid morning became hot enough to fry bacon.

Later in the afternoon, when the sails caught enough air, Ike attempted to fly a spinnaker. The spinnaker accidently fell in the ocean and became waterlogged, making it difficult to lift. We raced to the bow. After much tugging, the red, blue and white spinnaker was out of the water and billowing in the wind. The wind picked up and Ike turned off the engine. Around three the wind strengthened and became too strong for the spinnaker. Ike rushed to take the spinnaker down, but a gust of wind ripped the sheet from his hands and dumped it in the sea.

"Shit!" he shrieked. "The sheet's caught in the propeller." He recoiled in horror and the blood drained from his face. Trembling, he pulled off his shirt, grabbed his snorkel and mask and jumped overboard. I let out a strangled cry.

Shivering with fear, I held my breath. Without the engine and sails, I had no way of retrieving Ike if the boat moved off. The boat lurched forward while the spinnaker, sounding like pistol shots, flapped wildly. Gray breaking waves leapt up at *Osprey* like a school of attacking sharks.

Ike clung to the boat with his head underwater and released the sheet. "It's free!" he gasped. Then collapsed aboard and groaned. "I'm exhausted!" We began to wrestle with the snapping spinnaker. Getting it under control felt like taming a team of wild horses. Twenty minutes later the spinnaker was finally out of the water and stowed in its bag.

Ike turned the ignition key to start the engine. Nothing happened. "Shit!" he snapped, his eyes wide in alarm. "Not now!" He tried again—silence. He looked about wildly. The boat wallowed when waves broke against the hull.

After ten minutes of frenzied prodding, the engine coughed and started. We let out a simultaneous sigh of relief and motored the rest of the way. We arrived at the Fort Pierce inlet at dusk. It had been a long, hard day and we were exhausted. We anchored in an inlet close to the Intercoastal Waterway, and had no trouble falling asleep.

"I had a strange dream," Ike said looking puzzled at sunup. "A woman came to this island and asked to be taken to a great island in the west. The people there took her to He-Who-Lives-On-Water. He-Who-Lives-On-Water was afraid of her, for she was very beautiful. "I am just a humble fisherman!" he said, but he agreed to take her to this island in the west.

Waking one night on the boat, he saw that she was gone. He was afraid, but in the morning she was there. This happened the next night also. At sunrise he asked her, "Where do you go at night?"

"Be not afraid, I am a spirit woman, and I must walk with the moon," she replied. "I am She-Who-Walks-With-The-Moon. When we get to the great island in the west I will be yours forever." And so it came to pass.

"Is it about us?" I asked. Ike shrugged and smiled.

I returned to Macon, but Ike continued to motor-sail up the intercoastal waterway to Norfolk, Virginia. We had talked about my joining him there, but with our turbulent relationship, it seemed easier to part.

When I arrived home, I discovered that Wayne had kept my house and yard well maintained and had even stocked the kitchen with groceries.

What happens after sailing the ocean? What happens when rivers reach the sea? They rise as vapor to become drops for streams making their way to the sea. All things seem to start small, grow big and get small again. Man, animals, atoms even stars. Before a star collapses into a white dwarf, neutron shower or black hole, it becomes a red giant. And so it was with me. I'd fulfilled my lifelong dream to sail and live in the temple of the outdoors. I'd taken risks and survived. I'd proven that the universe is kind and Great Spirit cares. My self esteem was high, but my euphoria wasn't to last. At the height of my success, my ego was smashed.

I did not work for the remaining year, for I had cashed in some tax deferred savings to live on. The delight of being free to play for seven months turned into a nightmare. With no career and with my sailing adventure behind me, I felt adrift. Others seemed focused on their work and making money. With no one to spend time with, my life began to feel empty. This lack of purpose helped me understand why people get sick and die shortly after they retire.

Miles, a friend, asked me to canoe with him and his friend, Jon. Anxious to get back into the outdoors, I accepted. Jon, who was in his forties, looked like a blonde Greek god.

"I'm a white man on the outside but an Indian inside," he said, looking at me appraisingly with dreamy blue eyes. "The outdoors is my temple."

"You sound like me," I sighed, feeling an unwelcome warmth about my heart. He seemed dangerously attractive, but I felt drawn to him like a praying mantis meeting its death in order to mate.

He lived with his brother near Atlanta, where he had started a business leasing out closed circuit televisions for security purposes. Although he had a law degree he had previously sold mobile homes for a living.

We spent time together, but I felt uneasy. It bothered me that he had been married four times and had been dishonest and unfaithful with his mates. He spoke wistfully of being rejected by his lover and true soul-mate after a year-long affair while they were both married to others.

"The relationship taught me the importance of honesty," he said sadly.

Jon showered me with gifts, books, T-shirts and cards. "You're a spirit almost identical to myself," he said with a dimpled smile. "Our relationship is meant to be." His movie star looks and mystical language dazzled me. I, too, wanted to be his true soulmate. He wrote in one of his cards, "The universe in its infinite wisdom has brought us together and is giving us a time of being. It is not significant that we count hours, nor days, nor years. Love would not have itself be limited by such superficial demarcations, for it is forever complete unto itself." Blinded by his charms, I did not see that his love letters held no commitment and were not specific to me.

"You're so special, I could never lie to you," he whispered daily on the phone from work, speaking of a future together. By July Jon was living with me. Because he was struggling financially, I asked him to contribute only to food and utilities. He agreed but made no payments.

I began to feel like a drug. He'd act agitated until we'd made love each morning and evening. My urologist was mystified, for I had developed a chronic bladder infection although my cystoscope and MRI were normal.

"Please don't seduce me!" I pleaded with Jon. "I'm in pain."

"You'll get used to it," he growled. I gave in—my fear of losing him was greater than my pain. It seemed I no longer owned my body.

"I need to use a diaphragm," I said one morning when we began making love.

"Wait," he snarled holding me closer with a half smile.

"Jon, I'll get pregnant," I cried as I pushed to get out from under him. His smile broadened while he pinned me down harder.

"All that energy exploding like a volcano," he murmured, finally releasing me.

"You raped me!" I spat.

"I got excited!" he whispered pulling me into his arms. My anger dissipated but I felt trapped and worthless. He began to come home later and have more business engagements on weekends.

"Jon, is there someone else?" I asked nervously.

"I could never leave you," he said curtly.

"Jon is seeing another woman," Miles told me in October while Jon was away. I was stunned. When I confronted Jon on the phone, he denied it but became angry when he realized I knew. There were no apologies.

Four months later he wrote: "It is ironic that my relationship with you and Sue came into being literally within days of each other and that she knew about you almost from the very beginning." He went on: "Our relationship did not succeed or fail because of her existence....simple honesty in relationships with women has been one of the core lessons of my present incarnation....I am sorry for the pain I brought you."

He had molded himself into what he thought I wanted, and I'd sacrificed my soul for an illusion. Before my relationship with Jon, I had difficulty understanding people who commit murder. Now I knew that if I had owned a gun and had access to him when I discovered his betrayal, I think I would have killed him.

I'd taken risks; sailed and canoed with strangers, backpacked alone, but the real danger had lurked in my house and slept in my bed. I was shattered. Never again would I be so trusting.

Sex is a wonderful gift, but Jon had introduced me to the dark side of sex. If it had happened when I was in my twenties I don't know if I would have recovered.

My role as a counselor and giver was gone. My soul felt battered and it took many months to heal. I felt like an open wound—bleeding, raw and hurting.

Helping hands came from everywhere—friends, neighbors, former co-workers and family. Through their support I learned to receive Great Spirit's kindness. My mother called from South Africa for the first time in fifteen years.

"Get on a plane immediately," she urged. "The swine sounds dangerous." Although it would be three years more before I actually visited, her concern touched me.

As I became painfully aware of my weaknesses; my vulnerability to manipulation and my capability of murder, my empathy for others deepened. My health returned and I have not had a bladder infection since. My body seemed wiser than I—it knew the relationship was toxic.

Like wheat for bread, life gathered, thrashed, sifted, ground and kneaded me—hopefully life's fire would also strengthen and heal me. My crumbled ego was opening me to the Will of God. Before becoming selfless we need a self, for it is hard for God to use the weak and undeveloped. I also learned that when I am open to Spirit things seem easier, but when things go awry I am often on the wrong path. As I turned inward; with nothing to prove, the world shifted from being "I and me" to "us and we."

What happened to my friends?

Joe brought his boat back from the Bahamas in late 1992. He said he got hit by lightning off the coast of Georgia and that the navigation equipment was burned. In February 1995 he wrote; "I just completed a thousand-mile kayak race from Chicago to New York and came in ninth out of twenty-five." He said he would be marrying the woman who handled the press coverage in September and invited me to the wedding.

Doc, my Suwannee River canoe partner, is still around, and we travel together often. He also refers to our Suwannee trip as a powerful spiritual experience.

Wayne moved to Oregon to work at another Mental Health Center, and I've lost contact with Eddie and Jay.

Jeff and John, my ex-husbands, do keep in touch. Jeff left his teaching position at the law school to become a photographer in North Carolina. While doing a photo documentary with hospice patients and their families, he fell in love with the work, went back to school, and is now a hospice social worker in up-state New York. He remarried and is a practicing Zen Buddhist.

John moved to North Georgia to build and run an art gallery. He later remarried and now works as a family therapist on the Georgia coast.

Ike built a successful retail business in Norfolk, Virginia over the next two years. He asked me to marry him and to set sail for the Caribbean when he sold his business the following year. I agreed, and we began to date long distance.

While we were camping in the North Carolina mountains one night, there was a strange flickering light. Ike broke out into a sweat and began to shiver. I'd never seen Ike so traumatized and became concerned. He confided that he'd seen a similar light outside his cabin one winter night in New Hampshire. He'd put on his bathrobe and stepped outside the backdoor to investigate and suddenly had the impression he was being lifted into the air. His next memory was of lying on the couch in the livingroom. Although he was skeptical about aliens and UFO's, he had a vague feeling he had been abducted. When he got up he found the back door open.

"Would it help to go to a motel?" I volunteered.

"No, it won't," he groaned. "They can get you anywhere."

The rumble of thunder broke the silence. Realizing the lightning from an approaching storm was responsible for the flickering light, Ike calmed down and fell asleep. Ike's panic made me curious about the existence of aliens. I'd spent a lot of time alone in the woods and wondered why I had not been visited.

A couple of weeks later I watched a TV docudrama about a skeptical psychiatrist who had two female patients claim to have been abducted and impregnated by aliens. Both stated their fetuses were ripped from their bodies just before birth. I called Ike and told him to watch the show. He said he had already tried but found it too painful. According to the program aliens have targeted, studied and been involved with certain people and their families over a number of generations. Researchers suspect that the aliens impregnate and collect semen from chosen females and males to start a half human, half alien race on another planet. Victims often have memories of multiple encounters and have formed support groups to deal with their trauma. The experience with Ike led me to be more open to the possibility of UFO's.

When Ike sold his business a year later I did not accompany him on the sailboat. We realized it was his dream, not mine, and I feared more emotional struggles.

While visiting Venezuela Ike met a law student called Gley. They continued to date long distance when he settled in Puerto Rico two years later to start another retail business.

In the spring of 1997 he called me, "She's dead!" he wept. Between sobs he said she had been one of a handful of people killed in an earthquake when an office building collapsed in Venezuela. He could not stop crying and had not been able to eat or sleep for two days. They were going to get engaged when she visited him that summer.

"Three days ago I had a strong urge to get out her pictures and study them," he said hoarsely. "The Eagles song, *Everything Can Change in a New York Minute,* was playing when I began to cry without knowing why." When he heard about the earthquake in her home town the following day, he called her family and found she had died about the time he had studied her photographs. "How can I stop the hurt?" he wailed. "You're a counselor; you know about these things."

"You can't stop the pain, you go through it," I consoled. "It's like riding out a storm."

"But I didn't even get to say goodbye," he lamented.

"Ike, I know you don't believe in life after death, but I do—you can say goodbye now."

"You think so!"

"Yes."

"I'll try." A couple of days later he called. "You won't believe this. I got out her picture after talking to you and she appeared," he said triumphantly. "She looked like a transparent Native American dreamcatcher." She told him she had no brain and that she could not remember her past.

"I've got a brain; come join me," Ike offered after trying unsuccessfully to jog her memory. Ike said she moved behind him and entered at the base of his head. "I felt immediate peace," he said wistfully.

Having her spirit was both comforting and comical. When he took a shower that night she said, "Ah, a man's body!" She commented on his thoughts, and he discovered he could suddenly speak Spanish fluently.

I heard from Ike frequently over the next couple of weeks. His taste in food changed, and he had a burning desire to visit Gley's family in Venezuela. He also realized he had never grieved about his father's death when he was nine, and now he felt a deep compassion for people who had lost loved ones.

Gley's presence began to fade over the next year. Ike said he continues to feel her spirit, but it is more subtle now. He remains an atheist. Ike's experience made me wonder about life after death and to see that it is far more complex than I realized. Ike hopes to sell his store in a couple of years and sail to the Pacific islands.

Thousands of tired, nerve-shaken people are beginning to find out that going to the mountains is going home; that wilderness is necessary ... .
John Muir

CHAPTER 18

SYNCHRONICITIES

No bigger in the mass of the body than the thumb of a man, the Purusha, the Spirit within, is seated for ever in the heart of all creatures.

The Upanishads

In the last twenty years I have come to see what I thought was luck or an accident was not a coincidence at all. Carl Jung actually coined the word "synchronicity" for circumstances that seemed beyond chance.

Synchronicity seemed to be involved when I discovered I had an irregular heartbeat in 1994 and just "happened" to see a physician who had the same condition. He said he'd spent a fortune getting a diagnosis and found out his problem was benign. He refused to let me pay for my office visit.

Synchronicities are often involved when a misfortune turns out to be a blessing. I had a lot of losses in my childhood: living in different homes, having to leave people I loved; yet the pain I carried led to a satisfying career as a children's therapist.

My family's tendency to be frugal was often embarrassing. When I lived with my grandmother, we had no car; a bed in the living room was our couch, and we had minimal luxuries. Yet it was my family who taught me how to save, to live on half my income, and never to borrow money or pay interest. When I bought my first house, I had it paid for in three years. My car was bought with savings. I'm blessed that walking in the woods and swimming in rivers (which are free), hold more allure for me than commercial entertainment.

There were synchronicities when I bought my house in 1985. I told a real estate agent that I'd like a house around forty-five thousand dollars on a lake or river and I could make a ten-thousand dollar deposit.

"You can't get a house on water at that price," he scoffed. Three months later he called. "I got your house!" he blurted. It was a contemporary, with huge windows overlooking a lake and hardwood trees. The cost and downpayment was exactly what I requested and I could assume a VA loan. It was perfect! Thirteen years later I sold the house in three weeks at a profit.

The purchase of my next home had even more synchronicities. Before buying my first house Jeff, my ex-husband, and I sold a seventeen-acre tract of land we had bought in 1977. It was a little paradise with beautiful hard wood trees bordering a mountain-like creek. We sold it seven years later to a couple who planned to build a log cabin on the hill overlooking the creek.

I awoke one night in a cold sweat. What had I done? How could I have let the land go? The only consolation was that Jeff and I retained the title until the couple paid the money we had financed.

Then I got a second chance. While building the log cabin, the husband became a paraplegic after abdominal surgery. Although the house was completed by a contractor, the couple's marriage folded. When they paid the money they owed us, they let me buy back five acres with water frontage. Although saddened by their misfortune, I was overjoyed to have part of the land returned.

The wife got the house with five acres in the divorce settlement. When she moved out of state the husband, who was confined to a wheel chair, got life-time rights to live in the cabin. Since her husband needed money, he sold his seven acres with the wife's well and driveway to another couple with perpetual rights. I visited with him when I checked on my land. He had retired and was writing a book which he later self published.

When the cabin with huge windows overlooking the hardwood trees became rental property after his death, I longed to buy the house and the other five acres, but builders advised that the house's workmanship was sub-standard and not worth the asking price. The house is made out of those small round landscaping timbers normally used for flower beds. It has no central heat or air-conditioning, only a woodburning stove, a couple of propane heaters and an attic fan. The cabin remained rental property, but I continued to feel I belonged there. Then a series of coincidences led me back.

Bud Queen, a man who got my name from Doc and was new in town, called for information on the Macon Wilderness Club. When he heard I was leading a backpacking trip to the Georgia mountains a few weeks later he signed up and we car pooled together. He told me he was looking for property in a certain area. It just so happened that it was where my five acres was located. Upon hearing the coincidence, and without missing a beat, he declared, "Well, why don't I marry you so I don't have to look anymore?" Not knowing what the future held, I laughed.

A couple of years later the ex-wife got the house and land reappraised, and to her dismay discovered that it was depreciating. Being constructed out of landscaping timbers, having the well and driveway on someone else's property and having no central heat and air had hurt its value. She came down in price, and Bud and I (we'd been dating for two years) bought it when we got married in May 1998.

My two-year courtship with Bud made me realize he was the life partner I could grow old with. We're such opposites and he's so different from anyone I'd dated, I hardly recognized him as a mate. Unlike my past companions, he had a stable work history as a Contracting Officer for the National Guard. Not being a fan of the military, I assumed our values were worlds apart. I was wrong. Secondly, he's a deer hunter. Since wild animals are sacred I had to stretch to understand how hunters can shoot that which they love. My life-style is one of voluntary simplicity; he buys the best he can afford. "I can't ride in your Cadillac," I joked. "It would hurt my image!" He is a Southern Baptist; I am a mystic who attends church in nature's majestic cathedral; he thinks more like a Republican, I more like a Democrat; yet there is harmony, maturity, integrity, love and laughter in our relationship. What we share is a love for people and the great outdoors. Our differences bring us together rather than push us apart, and we have broadened our worlds to include each other. For the first time I can see how mates stay together, and I have the opportunity to break the pattern of losing loved ones that started in my childhood.

My career had come full circle. Seven months after I returned from the sailing trip, I started counseling children at the same clinic, but as a part time consultant. Working two or three days a week I felt that my life was more balanced. There was time for household chores, being with friends, working on creative projects and spending time outdoors. With the freedom to set my own hours, work became play. While my colleagues yearned for retirement, I was content.

Having a small income in a society that values money and possessions, I tried to focus on mentors such as Jesus, Buddha, St. Francis, Ghandi and Mother Theresa, all of whom owned little and gave much. With part time work my identity became more tied up with helping others than with a career. Consequently the stress from politics at work affected me less. However, when I did feel tension, I drew strength from my spirit quest insight that evil is necessary on earth to teach us unconditional love.

Now, five-and-a-half years later, I've decided to devote my time to a small private counseling practice and to writing and doing hospice volunteer work.

My encounter with God in the wilderness has changed my thinking to a more ecological spirituality and made the earth's history and her story of great interest.

Fossil records and contemporary molecular biology show that the universe is very old, around fifteen billion years, and that mankind is very young, around a million years. Mammals have been around less than one billion years. Dinosaurs roamed the earth only two hundred and thirty million years ago, and manlike creatures ten million years ago. In one million years humankind has managed to overpopulate the world with six-billion people and become toxic to the earth. (The earth had just over one-and-a-half billion people one hundred years ago.)

Religion and science can no longer be separate. God is not "out there" somewhere, but in the soil, in the trees and in ourselves. It's no accident that seventy-one percent of our substance consists of salty water, just as seventy-one percent of the earth is covered by ocean, that the genetic instructions or DNA molecule in human beings and other biological forms on the earth are written in the same language with the same code book, and that every woman's womb restages the drama of the origin of life in the gestation of every embryo.

Yet the stability of the world's climate remains at risk, half the shorelines are dying, coral reefs are sick everywhere, and large numbers of ocean fish and land animals have significantly decreased or disappeared. Environmentalists warn that the planet's water and air are being systematically poisoned by human wastes and ask that we stop destroying the world, for there is no place to which we can retreat, no planet in outer space that can provide refuge. If we continue to overpopulate and destroy Mother Earth by eliminating her animals and forests, polluting her water and air, we too will become extinct.

We have the technology to clean up our water and air. Instead, we allow our valuable natural resources and public health standards to be set by corporate profit margins. Large companies have successfully lobbied to stop municipal transportation. Although three-fifths of the air pollution in the United States comes from one-fifth of our present-day cars, the large steel-car industries and our fifty billion dollars a year oil industry are successfully lobbying against ultralight electric cars and other forms of renewable-energy transportation.

People of faith, whether they are Christian, Buddhist, Hindu, Islam or Jewish, need to meditate on the history of humankind, the earth and the universe. Our universe is only one among billions of universes. God is not one million years old, like us. We are not the first to be made in God's image. God's Spirit is in the whole of creation, and everything has divine power.

The Western tradition looks down on nature by emphasizing original sin. It is an insult to God, the creator of our fifteen-billion-year-old universe. Sin originated with one million-year-old man. The time has come to see the beauty, wonder and grace in God's creation. Mother Earth and her inhabitants are our teachers; the fifty-six million year old whale is our elder. We need to take care of all creation—the plants, animals and people—for the earth is sacred and nature is a doorway to enter the spiritual realm.

I now know that spending time in nature is not just another approach to fulfillment. Connecting with the body of the earth is our birthright and our salvation.

Credits

The author thanks the following publishers and individuals for permission to reprint copyrighted material.

Excerpts from *Talking with Nature* 1987 by Michael J. Roads. Reprinted by permission of H J Kramer, P.O. Box 1082, Tiburon, CA 94920.

Excerpts from the video *Canticle of the Cosmos* 1990 by Brian Swimme. Reprinted by permission of the Tides Foundation.

Excerpts from *The Power of the Myth* 1988 by Joseph Campbell. Reprinted by permission of Doubleday, a division of Randam House, Inc.

Excerpts from *The Drama of the Ocean* 1976 by Elizabeth Borgese. Reprints by permission of Harry N. Abrams, Inc. Publishers.

Excerpts from *Creation Spirituality* 1991 by Matthew Fox. Reprinted by permission of *Resurgence Magazine.*

Maps courtesy of *Custom Mapping Services,* John A. Cleaveland. 16 Creekview Lane, Durham NC 27705-5581. (919) 489-1837

ORDER FORM

EARTH, THE FORGOTTEN TEMPLE

Telephone or fax orders: (912) 992-9063
Mail orders: *Impala Press*
      1387 Boxankle Road
      Forsyth, GA 31029

Ship to:
Name_____
Address_____
City_____State_____Zip_____
Telephone_____

Please send:
_____books at $12.95, $_____
Shipping and handling
(Add $3.00 for first book, $.75 per additional book)
$_____
Total
$_____

Niki will do talks and slide presentations about her outdoor and spiritual adventures. She also does workshops on *The Healing Power of Wild Places* and *Using the Healing Power of Nature in Counseling.* To inquire about scheduling a talk or workshop call 912-992-9063.